DAVID VAL

by

DAVE AUXIER, DVM

Edited by Randall E. Auxier, PhD

To Linda & Robert,
oth nks for your interest
in Auxier genealogy
and history

Dave Auxier
Aug 16, 2010

1

DAVID VALENTINE'S DAY

ISBN: 1452830142

Dave Auxier
5612 Country Club Rd.
Murphysboro, IL 62966

THE AUTHOR

Dave Auxier is a retired veterinarian presently living in Murphysboro, Illinois. He is a graduate of Berea College, Berea, Kentucky, with a Bachelor of Science Degree in Agriculture, and Auburn University, Auburn, Alabama, with a Doctor of Veterinary Medicine Degree. He practiced for 42 years in Kentucky and Tennessee.

Dave is married to the former Eileen Gunter, a church musician and founder of the Kindermusik Program at the University of Memphis. They have two children, Ann Auxier Bowsher of Memphis, and Randall E. Auxier of Murphysboro.

OTHER BOOKS BY THE AUTHOR
(All self-published)

The Cornhuskers (1977)

The Auxier Family (Genealogy, 1995)

The Auxier Family, Second Edition, (2000)

The Ancestors and Descendants of John Lorenzo Gunter and Eulala Moore Gunter (Genealogy, 2005)

DEDICATION

Henry Preston Scalf (1902-1979)

This book is dedicated to the memory of Henry Scalf, noted author, teacher, editor, and historian. Mr. Scalf was for many years the editor of *The Floyd County Times* in Prestonsburg, Kentucky. This gifted man wrote extensively about the history of Eastern Kentucky, and in particular about the men who served in the Civil War. He had knowledge about the life and death of my namesake great, great uncle, Captain David Valentine Auxier that was not available from any other source, and I am deeply indebted to him for providing valuable source material for this book

...Dave Auxier

ACKNOWLEDGEMENTS

A posthumous "thank you" goes to Henry Scalf to which this book is dedicated. Henry was not only the source for much of the information about David Valentine's final days on earth, but also for the wealth of historical perspective on the culture and people of Eastern Kentucky during the Civil War. His contributions in this regard were enormous.

I would also like to express my appreciation to John David Preston for his comprehensive history of the Civil War in the Big Sandy Valley, first written in 1984 and re-issued with additional information in 2008. I have quoted from his scholarly research extensively in the chapters which deal with the buildup and prosecution of the great internecine conflict of the 1860's.

Thanks also go to all the authors of books and articles about the Battle of Saltville, Virginia, which claimed my great, great uncle's life. I drew a great deal of information and inspiration from those writings.

Kudos to Robert M. Baker and Brian E. Hall for their splendid CD-ROM on the 39th Kentucky Mounted Infantry, U. S. Volunteers, which was David Valentine's regiment.

My son, Randall E. Auxier, editor of the prestigious Library of Living Philosophers at Southern Illinois University, took time out of his very busy schedule to edit this volume and advise me on style as well as substance. I am grateful for his expert assistance.

Finally, I would like to thank my wife Eileen for supporting me in all my genealogical and historical endeavors. She realized how important these projects were to me and to the Auxier family as a whole.

TABLE OF CONTENTS

Title page .... Page   1
Author... Page   3
Other Books by the Author .... Page   4
Dedication .... Page   5
Acknowledgements .... Page   7
Table of Contents .... Page   9
Citations and Abbreviations .... Page   11
Preface .... Page   13

Chapter I   The Legend .... Page   15
Chapter II   Connections .... Page   19
Chapter III   Roots .... Page   27
Chapter IV   Reasons .... Page   43
Chapter V   To Arms .... Page   49
Chapter VI   Prison .... Page   59
Chapter VII   The French Lady .... Page   65
Chapter VIII Return to Action .... Page   73
Chapter IX   Saltville .... Page   81
Chapter X   Casualty .... Page   91
Chapter XI   Lost and Found .... Page   99
Chapter XII   Found Again................................ Page   107
Chapter XIII Relocation.................................. Page   113
Chapter XIV Countdown .... Page   123
Chapter XV   David Valentine's Day .... Page   129

Epilogue .... Page   151
Bibliography .... Page   155
Appendix .... Page   161

CITATIONS AND ABBREVIATIONS

39th KY	*39th Kentucky Mounted Infantry*
AF	*The Auxier Family, 1995*
AF-2	*The Auxier Family, 2000*
AH	*Auxier History, 1755 – 1908*
AH–R&A	*Auxier Family History, Revisions and Additions*
AH-ADD	*Addendum to Auxier History*
ALB	*From Albig to Auxier (Wells)*
ARM	*From Armsheim to Auxier (Wells)*
BOONE	*Boone: A Biography*
BSR	*Biographical Sketches and Records*
BSV	*The Big Sandy Valley*
CONNELLEY	*The Founding of Harman's Station*
CW–BSV	*The Civil War in the Big Sandy Valley*
CW-DBD	*The Civil War, Day by Day*
CWH	*Civil War Hostages*
CWP	*Civil War Prisons*
CWT	*Civil War Times Illustrated*
DVA	*Capt. David Valentine Auxier, USA, Scalf*
FCT	*Floyd County Times (Scalf)*
FILSON	*Filson Historical Society*
FOSTER	*Prisoner Exchange Cartel explained.*
JCK	*A Brief History of Johnson County, Kentucky*
JWC	*Jenny Wiley Country*
KA	*Kentucky Archives, Johnson County Vital Statistics*
KHS	*Kentucky Historical Society, Vouchers*

LC	*Lawrence County, A Pictoral History*
LMOW	*Like Men of War: Black Troops in the Civil War*
MEM	*Memorial Service for David Valentine Auxier, 1961*
OM	*Our Memories of the Civil War Linger Scalf*
OR	*Official Records of the War of the Rebellion*
OR-C	*Compendium of the War of the Rebellion*
PGP	*Pennsylvania German Pioneers*
PH	*The Paintsville Herald*
POW	*Prisoner of War Records*
RHE	*From Rheydt to Auxier (Wells)*
SM	*The Saltville Massacre*
SMF	*Stephen Meek Ferguson...* (Scalf)
SWV-CW	*Southwest Virginia in the Civil War*
USPO	*U.S. Pension Office*
W-SWV	*The War in Southwest Virginia*
ZAR	Zarvona - *The French Lady*

PREFACE

I will admit that I struggled with this book for nineteen years before finishing it in 2010. The project was placed on hold several times due to more pressing responsibilities such as the compilation of two genealogy books and the organization of four family reunions. During those respites, there was always the feeling that there was a karmic debt that needed to be paid.

I was born in Nebraska where Dad and Mom farmed for twenty-three years, but my teen years were spent in Eastern Kentucky near where David Valentine lived. During my time in the mountains, I got a pretty good feel for the region and for the Auxier families who descended from David's generation.

I am pleased to present at long last, a biographical novella about a Civil War hero who languished for 126 years in almost total obscurity in an abandoned hillside cemetery in Virginia. We have a revival of a family legend when his bones were retrieved from a desolate gravesite and moved to his family cemetery in Kentucky. We have a solemn memorial service with military honor guard to commemorate the relocation, which in turn led to a renewed interest in the life and times of Captain David Valentine Auxier.

Finally, I have, by writing this book, unburdened myself of that haunting feeling that I had some ethereal debt to pay. I have believed for some time that I am inexorably connected to the essence of my namesake great, great uncle, and I will try to convey what I mean by that as the story unfolds.

The Author

CHAPTER I

THE LEGEND

My name is Charles David Auxier. My mother and father collaborated on my given names. The "Charles" came from my mother's older brother, Charlie, one of mom's favorites whose life was cut short by tuberculosis. The "David" came from my dad's side of the family. His great uncle, David Valentine Auxier, also lost his life at an early age, but under completely different circumstances.

David Valentine was killed in the Civil War at the age of 24, a fact which became a mixed bag of sorrow, pride and mystery as the story was told and re-told around family hearths and dinner tables in the decades following that fateful event in 1864. Most of what I learned about my hero uncle came from my dad, Earl, who was an avid reader, especially about history, and in particular about the Civil War. He could hold forth in great detail about the major battles of the war, with the names of the opposing generals, the tactical situations, and the reasons for victory or defeat.

Dad was born in Johnson County, Kentucky, and at the age of twenty-six followed his great uncles (David Valentine's brothers) to Nebraska. He dreamed of emulating their success as farmers, bankers, and state legislators in the fertile plains of Richardson County in the southeast corner of the state. Dad's future as a farmer and logger in the rugged mountains of Eastern Kentucky looked dismal, so he relocated his young family to what he hoped would be a better opportunity in the West.

Earl Auxier as a young man

Things never quite worked out the way my father envisioned. All of the homestead land had been gobbled up by the time he arrived in 1917.   Initially, Dad worked as a farm hand for other land-owners, and after a few years, managed to rent 160 acres and a large house on a farm near the town of Verdon.in the same area his great-uncles had settled thirty years earlier.   Prospects for success looked good for my father during the 1920's, but the Great Depression with all its misery was just around the corner. Droughts, dust storms, and the failing economy made it impossible for my father to get ahead. He was a hard worker and wanted desperately to provide a good life for his family, but the best he could do during 23 years in Nebraska was to remain a sharecropper. The family never went hungry because we always had a good garden, and Mom was a wizard at canning and preserving. Dad put meat on the table by butchering a hog or a steer during the winter. There weren't many tangibles to show for his efforts, but as with so many others in similar circumstances, we children later took pride in the character that we cultivated during those lean years.

The David Valentine story came up from time to time and I was fascinated by how the twenty-two year old had volunteered in a Union regiment, fought in numerous skirmishes, was captured by Confederate militia, and was later released under a prisoner exchange program. After rejoining his unit, he was mortally wounded at the battle of Saltville, Virginia.   I learned that he was buried in a small family cemetery on the battlefield, and that the location of the grave was unknown to the family for almost 70 years.

By 1940, Dad's back problems forced him to give up large scale farming in Nebraska, but these stories about David Valentine were repeated to me by other family members after we returned to Kentucky. The old home place in Johnson County was vacant after my grandfather Auxier moved into Paintsville, the county seat.   Mom and Dad and the three youngest children, myself included, went to live on a run-down 77 acre farm on top of a 120 foot cliff. There was no decent road to the old clapboarded log house. That was to be the family home for the next 25 years. Only about 7 acres of the "farm" were level enough for cultivation, but Dad's health was not good enough for more than that anyway. He and Mom, with some help from my brother Bob and me, managed to make a living by peddling vegetables in town, raising a small acreage of burley tobacco, and selling a few calves every year. 1 Life in the mountains was difficult, but just as in Nebraska, we developed even more of that thing called character.

Dad, Mom, and the author, about 1943

I began to feel a sense of pride for having been given the name of one of our family heroes. The Auxiers had furnished untold numbers of soldiers and sailors for military conflicts as far back as the Revolutionary War, but to my knowledge, no one in our immediate family line had lost his life in battle, apart from the uncle whose name I carried. So, the legend of David Valentine had a certain mystique. In my youthful imagination I wondered what he was like in personality and demeanor and how he felt about the war that he was drawn into. These questions were answered in large part many years later as I read his personal letters and the writings of others who recounted the events of his brief military service.

I was aware that the Auxier family had been among the earliest settlers in the Big Sandy Valley, and that Daniel Boone

---

1 We transported calves to market in the family car by taking out the back seat and wrapping the calf's hind quarters in a burlap bag to prevent fouling the interior of the car.

had spent part of one winter at the home of Samuel and Sarah Auxier, my 4th great grandparents. I knew there had been many lawyers, judges and teachers among our ancestors, and that my own great grandfather, George Washington Auxier, who had been in David Valentine's unit in the war, had served as sheriff of Johnson County. One hundred twenty years later, he was voted one of the 10 most influential men in the history of the county.

In my early years in Eastern Kentucky, I would never have dreamed that in 1990, at the age of 59. I would be the last in a succession of relatives to find David Valentine's grave. I was last for reasons I will explain in due course.

CHAPTER II

CONNECTIONS

Why was I compelled by some unseen force to write this book? As I mentioned in the preface, there has been for a very long time a nagging consciousness that I was connected to David Valentine Auxier in ways other than genealogically. For me, the story begins with David Valentine's brother, George Washington Auxier, who was my great grandfather. The following biography is taken from an addendum to an unpublished 1908 history of the Auxier family by Agnes Auxier. It was written around 1960 by an unknown author:

> "George Washington [Auxier], son of Nathaniel and Hester Ann Mayo Auxier, was born November 10, 1841, near the mouth of John's Creek in Floyd County, Kentucky. When a young boy, his father moved his family to the Blockhouse Bottom, just opposite East Point, where he built a large Colonial style house. It was one of the first houses in the Sandy Valley to have plastered walls. The plaster was brought up the Big Sandy River by flat boat.
>
> In George Washington's childhood, an artist of some note came to the home and painted the portraits of Presidents George Washington and Abraham Lincoln on the smooth white plastered walls where they remained in good condition until the year 1907, long after the house had been abandoned as a residence because of the belief that it was haunted.
>
> It was here he spent the days of his youth, going to school and helping his father and brothers with the farm work.
>
> George Washington was a handsome man, of fine stature, six feet tall, with high, broad forehead, black hair, and piercing black eyes. In later years he weighed

250 pounds. He, as well as his brothers and sisters were gifted with deep melodious voices. There being not much other form of entertainment at the time, the friends and neighbors would gather at their home to hear them sing hymns and songs popular at that time.

George Washington joined the 39th Kentucky Volunteers and was a sergeant in this company. He was with his brother, Captain David V. Auxier, at the battle of Saltville, Virginia, and saw him wounded in battle. He and some soldiers were able to get him to shelter in a barn nearby. Although being mortally wounded, he urged them back into battle. Later, when they were able to return, they found he had been taken to a residence where he died as a result of his wounds. He is buried in the old McCready Cemetery at Saltville.

On Dec. 3, 1865, George Washington was married to Angeline Prater, daughter of John and Jemima Auxier Prater at her home on Burning Fork, Magoffin County. The house in which they were married still stands and has been occupied by their descendants until about 1955. Still in the house is furniture

George Washington Auxier and Angeline

and articles used at that period of time.

The deaths of his parents left several unmarried brothers and sisters at home, Ed and Nat being only two and four years old. George Washington, as eldest brother, felt it was his duty to stay home and help provide for their welfare and education; therefore, he and his young wife, Ann, remained on the farm with them, being father and mother to them until they all grew up and married. Ed and Nat remained with them until the ages of twenty-one and twenty-five when they went to Nebraska.

How well George Washington and Ann performed their duty to these children was attested to by Ed Auxier later in life, when he said on the death of his brother, that they were very good parents to them and the only father and mother he and Nat ever knew. Of Ann, he said, 'She was the best woman that ever lived.'

After leaving the old homestead, they lived for the next few years in the vicinity of Hager Hill, where their daughters were born.

In 1881, George Washington moved with his family to Fish Trap on Big Paint Creek, Johnson County, where they lived the rest of their lives on a large farm in one of the most scenic sections of the county.

George Washington was a man of much ability and many interests. Here, he and his sons and brothers, Ed and Nat, operated the farm, raising tobacco, corn, cattle, and hogs. At the same time, he owned one of the few general stores in the county, having his merchandise brought up the Big Sandy River by steamboat from Cattlettsburg to Paintsville, from where it was hauled by oxen or mule team to his store at Fish Trap (later Manila, KY). Here, his customers would come by wagon, a distance of ten to twelve miles, bringing their families and their produce which they would exchange for farm machinery, household articles, dress goods, and groceries. The families would spend the day trading, visiting, and partaking of the good food prepared by his wife, Ann, and her daughters.

There was also a tannery on the place where hides were tanned and prepared for leather goods. Operation of this tannery ceased after one of the workmen was killed by lightning while at work.

George Washiungton was a Republican interested and well informed in politics. He was twice elected to the office of Sheriff of Johnson County, serving for a period of nine years. He was well educated for his day.

He had a very pleasing personality and was considered the best-known and popular man at the county at that time. He had a beautiful melodious singing voice and sang and played the violin and banjo with his sons as long as he lived. He was a member of the Masonic Lodge.

He and his wife were Methodists. They were very much interested in religion, very tolerant and helpful to all denominations. They were known for their good deeds and hospitality. One time when the United Baptist Church was holding its annual association nearby, they entertained more than one hundred people in their home, more than any of the Baptist brethren.

After this time, his health began to fail, and after an illness of two years, he succumbed to heart dropsy at the age of fifty-four. He was laid to rest in the cemetery on the hill overlooking their old home and farm.

There is a magnificent view from this cemetery, from which the hills of Paintsville can be seen in the distance seven miles away.

His wife Ann was of small stature, good looking, with dark complexion, soft brown eyes, and abundant black hair, which remained so until her death. She was intelligent, well read, possessed a remarkable memory, and many were the stories of pioneer and Civil War days she handed down to her children and grandchildren.

After the death of her husband, Ann carried on in the traditions of her ancestors being known for her kindness and good deeds for as long as she lived. She died of pneumonia on March 9, 1911 at the age of eventy, and was laid to rest alongside her husband at the cemetery on the hill." (AH-ADD4, 1-3)

So, my great grandfather, for whom I feel a great affinity, lived with his family on a farm at Fish Trap on the Big Paint Creek in Johnson County, Kentucky – the same place I grew up. The large two-story house stood in a field a few hundred yards from the edge of an enormous canyon through which Paint Creek flowed (and occasionally rampaged during spring floods). On the opposite cliff top was the smaller, more rugged farm which my father owned after he returned in 1940 from his years in Nebraska. 2

George Washington's old house was gone by 1940, but his youngest son, George Garfield Auxier, known in the family as "Uncle Garrie," had built an equally imposing home for his large family nearer the cliff's

edge. There was actually only a short distance between Uncle Garrie's house and that of my parents across the deep chasm. It was not difficult to converse in a loud voice from front porch to front porch.

Uncle Garrie Auxier and his wife, Lula

There are so many preternatural connections between my great grandfather and myself. Reading about my great grandfather is like reading a letter from home, since I am also a Methodist who has always been similarly active in civic life. I even play the banjo and guitar, and have a daughter named "Ann" who is in many ways similar to the descriptions given of my great grandmother, "Angeline." These may be coincidences, but then again, they may not be. Blood is thick as mud and genes are thicker still, and for all we know, the spirit of those hills recycles itself across chasms of time as well as space. I wouldn't want to overstretch my case, though. My great grandfather George was of fine

---

2 George W. Auxier was one of several men who were reported to have been ferry keepers and tavern owners on the Big Sandy River. The source did not make it clear which of the two endeavors Auxier was involved in. This would have been in the time period after the war and before George moved his family to the Paint Creek farm. (JCK, 12)

stature, with black hair and piercing black eyes. No one has ever used any of those words to describe me.

I remain intrigued by certain moments of "recognition," one might say. Why did the hair stand up on the back of my neck when in December, 1990, I found David Valentine's grave in Virginia and stumbled onto the small fieldstone with the name *"D. Auxier"* chiseled into it? Why do I choke up each time I tell that story and have to pause to regain my composure?

Finally, I think the real clincher is something that happened during a workshop on intuition that my wife Eileen and I attended in the late 1990's. One of the assigned exercises was designed to discover something about the nature of our core beliefs and habits. We paired off and practiced what has been called guided imagery. I happened to be partnered with an experienced psychologist who knew the right questions to lead me through the exercise. She first asked me if there was a particular time in history that I was attracted to or in which I had a strong interest. I responded that I, like my father, loved to read and hear about the Civil War and visit the important battlefields. She then asked if there were any family members who had participated in that war. Without hesitation, I gave a brief history of the military careers of David Valentine Auxier and his brother, George Washington Auxier. My partner sensed that she was onto something significant in my psyche, so she pressed for more details on the circumstances surrounding David's wounding and death. When I got to the part about George, my great grandfather, finding David mortally wounded and having to leave him due to the exigencies of the situation, I totally lost my composure and sobbed uncontrollably for a full ten minutes. It was a release of emotion that I had never experienced.

I have thought about that experience many times, and have deduced that there was a debt that was only partially repaid when in 1991 I relocated David Valentine's remains from the abandoned Virginia graveyard to his family cemetery back home in Johnson County, Kentucky. Now I had to write the story, not just for David Valentine, but also for my great grandfather George, and for me, if indeed a substantive distinction can be made in this scenario. Obviously, you, dear reader may draw your own conclusions. I have already drawn mine.

CHAPTER III

ROOTS

Before I come to the main narrative, it is important to say something about the family, how we have kept our own, and what traditions we observe. The Auxier family has been blessed with serious genealogists who have pored over untold numbers of census books, courthouse records, ship's manifests, military archives, Social Security records, cemetery burial lists, and family Bibles. It was thought for many years that the Auxiers were of French extraction, and I reported that belief in both editions of *The Auxier Family*, which I published in 1995 and 2000. (AF, 1995, AF2, 2000) Subsequent research has cast doubt on that tradition. The best information we now have suggests that the family descends from an area in what is now in the southwest corner of West Germany. Over the centuries, this region has often fallen into dispute over the boundaries between France and the Germanic countries that preceded the current national designation. Our progenitors may have spoken a dialect of German.

Agnes Auxier (1868 - 1924), a librarian, schoolteacher, and newspaper correspondent in Johnson County, Kentucky, wrote the first known history of the Auxier family in 1908. (AH)

Agnes Auxier
1868 - 1920

This remarkable lady persevered despite the affliction of deafness in her later years, and eventually died of tuberculosis.

Agnes made the possibly erroneous assumption that our roots were in the town of Auxerre, France, located about 75 miles southeast of Paris on the left fork of the Yonne River. (AH, 1)Numerous researchers, including some professional genealogists in France, have since tried with no success to link our heritage to this French provincial town. Given the limited access to records and archives, and the poor communications of her day, it is understandable why Agnes might have linked Auxerre with the *Auxier* spelling of the name that was adopted by most branches of the family after 1800 in the USA. But in any case, she gave us a wonderful historical and genealogical framework with which to work in later years. My 1995 edition of *The Auxier Family* was dedicated to Agnes Auxier. (AF, 1995)

Auxerre, France

In her 1908 work, Agnes Auxier identified a man named Michael Auxier (she used the Anglicized spelling) as the progenitor of the family. She said he was a Huguenot, born in Auxerre, France, who moved with his family to the province of Alsace in Eastern France, which was known to be a safer haven from the extreme persecution of the Huguenots by the Crown of France and the Catholic Church at that time. Agnes wrote that while in that location, Michael married a woman named Amelia Christopher, who lived in Southwest Germany, just across the Rhine River from Alsace. (AH, 1) It is unknown where Agnes got this information. It is unlikely that she simply made it up, but no source has yet been discovered.

There are some aspects of the early Auxier narrative that ring true. One of the more salient correlations was that Michael "Axer's" name did appear on the ship's passenger list of the Robert and Alice, Martley Cussack, Master, departing from Rotterdam, Holland, and arriving at the Port of Philadelphia on September 24, 1742. 3 There were 75 names listed, all of them male. It was apparently the custom of that era to list only the names of male passengers. (PGP, 330)

The theory of our family connection to France persisted unquestioned until the year 2000 when a cousin named John B. Wells III re-examined the lineage of the Auxier family and came to different conclusions about our country of origin. John is a certified genealogist whose family also lived in Johnson County, Kentucky. He discovered convincing evidence that he was a descendant of one of the daughters of Johann Michael Axer, whom he identifies with the Michael Auxier that Agnes Auxier had named as the progenitor of the Auxier family. (ARM, foreword, 1) Historical research never comes to incontrovertible conclusions, but I am persuaded by Wells's case. One simple point is that even Agnes Auxier refers to the father of the clan as "Michael," which is the German (and English) spelling, not as "Michel," the French equivalent.

---

3 Agnes Auxier wrote that Michael Axer arrived in Pennsylvania in 1755. (AH, 1)

Wells and other researchers also uncovered hard evidence that the Axer family emigrated from   a beautiful region of Southwest Germany not far from the French border. Since the border between France and Germany moved, depending on the victor and the vanquished in the most recent war in that location, it is difficult to draw stark lines between one group and the other –and after all, the dominant ethnicity of France and Germany is the same.

The region in Wells's account is called Rhineland Pfalz, and he found a number of records linking Johann Michael Axer's brother, Christian, to villages in that area. Michael's birthplace has not been officially documented, though his name does appear in church records in some of the same villages where Christian was known to have lived.

In 2001, John Wells led an entourage of 20 Auxier cousins on a tour of France and Germany, which included stops at Auxerre, France and Armsheim, Germany, the points of special interest for further research on the family history. 4 The group found Auxerre to be a beautiful old market city with a magnificent 13th century cathedral, but again, no obvious link to our family origins. Armsheim (which is about 20 miles southwest of Mainz), on the other hand, revealed significant pearls of great value in its archives relevant to the Axer name. This village was one of several in the area to be revisited by a second tour led by Wells in 2006. With copious notes in hand to circumstantially point to Southwest Germany as the Auxier family's European place of origin, John Wells still needed something to substantiate his theory. In 2003, he developed a project to prove his ideas through DNA testing. With hard evidence that one of our family's earliest ancestors, Christian Axer, was born in one of the small villages in Rhineland Pfalz and had married a woman in another nearby village, Wells decided to try to connect by DNA the descendants of Christian to those of Michael. Three male descendants from Christian's branch and two from Michael's line, all bearing the Axer,

_____

4 The author was a member of this entourage.

Auxer, Auxier, or Oxier name, were asked to provide DNA sample material for cross matching. The Y-chromosome markers used in the test matched perfectly for all five men. These tests proved conclusively that Michael and Christian were closely related. Assuming that the common male ancestor shared by all those tested was indeed an elder of Michael's and Christian's, the birth time line for the two suggested that they were brothers, or at least close cousins. The DNA test results demonstrated that there was no reason to doubt, at this point, that the Auxier family came to America from Southwest Germany. (RHE, 5)

Wells' findings were given even more credence during his second family heritage tour to the specific area of Germany where the Axer name had been found in previous research. John had made contact with some cousins bearing the Axer name who were living in the villages from whence Christian had immigrated to America in 1748. These newly discovered cousins guided the tour group to view ancient church records containing the names of Johann Michael, Johann Christian and several other family members dating back to the early 17th century. Wells, *et al*, was able to add three more generations to the known Axer genealogy. During the visit, the locals showed their American cousins some houses built in the mid 1700's with the Axer name engraved above the door. Some of these residences are still inhabited by Axer descendants.

John Wells names Friederich Axer as the earliest identified ancestor of what we can safely call the Axer/Auxer/Auxier/Oxier family. His exact birth date is unknown, but extrapolating from the known birth years of his sons, we can safely calculate that he was born around 1620 to 1625 in the Rheinische Palatinate, in what is now Germany. Wells speculates that Friederich was among the numerous families that moved from the Cologne area in the lower Rhine River Valley after the Thirty Years War (1618 - 1648). This region was known throughout Europe as a center for the textile industry. Several Axer males listed their occupation as linen weaver. Friederich's family settled in or near the village

31

of Albig in Rhineland Pfalz, and his two sons, Hans Peter Axer and Johannes Axer were born there in 1643 and 1645. (Ibid, 4)

The second and third generations after Friederich are well documented with the names Johannes and Friederich being repeated as was the custom in that day and time.

Johann Michael Axer, David Valentine's third, great grandfather, the first Axer known to immigrate to America, took the oath of allegiance to the British Crown in Pennsylvania on Sept. 24, 1742, the day he arrived at the Port of Philadelphia. He settled in the township of Tulpehocken in Lancaster County, Pennsylvania. No records have been found to establish his exact place of residence, or evidence that he owned property there, but the names of his family do appear in the archives of the Reformed Church in that location.

Contrary to Agnes Auxier's 1908 history, it seems Johann Michael did not marry before arriving in America. He may have been a "redemptioner," meaning he had to work a period of years to pay the cost of his passage across the Atlantic. He may indeed have been indentured to his future father-in-law, Ulrich Spiess, who arrived in Pennsylvania from Germany in 1734. Michael married Spiess' daughter, Maria Barbara, on December 21, 1746. (Ibid, 1) They had at least nine children, the first four of whom were born in Pennsylvania and the remainder in Virginia to which Johann Michael moved his family in the mid-1750's.

Aside from the fact that Johann Michael was the first known Auxier to arrive in America, he is also known for an incident that occurred near the end of his life. According to Agnes Auxier, Michael was stalking deer at a salt lick near Fort Blackmore, Virginia, when he was surprised by an Indian who knocked him senseless with a tomahawk and relieved him of his scalp. Miraculously, the wounds were not fatal. Michael was said to have worn a hat at all times thereafter to cover the horrible scars, and became known in family history as "Bald Headed Mike." (AH, 8)

Family historians have exulted in saying that all five of

Michael's sons served in the Revolutionary War. However, this claim cannot be validated because it is now believed that the two youngest sons, Michael II, and Abraham, would have been too young to serve in the war. Michael II's birth year is uncertain, and Abraham is thought to have been born around 1774. One of the older sons, Simon, was born about 1755 to 1757, and according to his own accounts, took part in numerous battles and campaigns of the Revolution. He said that he was with Gen. George Washington at Valley Forge, and participated in the battles of Trenton, Brandywine, Monmouth, Guilford Courthouse, and Yorktown. He asserted that he was at Yorktown when Gen. Cornwallis surrendered on Oct. 19, 1781. (Ibid, 7) None of these claims has been documented, but Simon's narrative has been passed down as fact for more than two centuries.

Samuel, one of the older sons of Johann Michael, and designated "Samuel I" because of the dozens of Samuels who descended from him, was a scout for the Continental Army, serving several short tours of duty spying on Indian activities in Southwest Virginia and Eastern Kentucky. It was during these trips into the wilderness that he met Mathias Harman, a fearless Indian fighter and frontiersman who had tried several times to establish a permanent settlement in the Big Sandy Valley of Kentucky. Indians had burned the settlers' cabins and in general made the area a dangerous and inhospitable place for the white man.

It was to one of these outposts, subsequently called Harman's Station, that Jenny Wiley made her way after escaping from several months of Indian captivity in 1790. This young mother from Southwest Virginia became a legend in folklore after surviving the horrible ordeal of having a mixed band of Indians break into her home, massacre her 15 year old brother and three of her children and drag her and her youngest child into the forest. That child, along with another who was born soon after Jenny was captured, was also murdered by her captors. The story of this young woman's bravery and resourcefulness has been recounted in many

33

books and plays, and in the 1950's, a State Park in Floyd County, Kentucky, was named in her honor.

Soon after Jenny Wiley's escape to Harman's Station near the mouth of John's Creek on the Big Sandy, the settlers were once again forced to leave because of Indian hostility. In 1791, Simon Auxier and Samuel I, were among those who accompanied Mathias Harman to rebuild the station. This time they built two strong connecting blockhouses, each about twenty feet square and two stories in height, with special features designed to help ward off Indian attacks. Walls and doors were of thick oak timbers, and the second stories projected out over the first story by two feet and were fitted with loopholes for firing down on any attacker who made it as far as the doors. Trees and bushes were cleared back the distance of a musket shot from the houses, and this riverside location became known as Harman's Station. (Connelley, pp 67-68) This riverside location later became known as the Blockhouse Bottom. Auxier descendants still own and live on portions of the original settlement.

After the Battle of Fallen Timbers in Ohio in 1794, the frontier areas of Kentucky, Indiana, and Ohio, was less dangerous, and settlers began pouring into the region. In 1795 alone, 75 new families arrived in the Big Sandy Valley. Among those was the family of Samuel Auxier I who paid the equivalent of $1,500.00 for a large section of the Blockhouse Bottom known as the Shepherd Claim, and brought his family across the mountains from Culpepper County, Virginia. The ownership of this land purchase had been misrepresented, and a few years later, Samuel's widow and sons had to pay the rightful owner the equivalent of $2,700.00 for the same property. 5(AH, 3)

Samuel I, and his wife Sarah Brown, had nine children, all but the youngest of whom were born in Virginia. Tragedy befell the family within a year after arrival in Kentucky when

34

---

5 The author has a photocopy of the claim that Samuel I filed.

their three-year old son, Elijah, disappeared from a canebrake near the Auxier homestead and was never found. Neighbors and family members searched desperately for a week, but never found a trace of the little fellow. Was he devoured by wild animals? Was he captured by Indians? Did he drown in the river? The mystery was never solved. (AH, 17-18)Samuel himself met an untimely death when he was killed at about age 40 in a horseback accident while on a buffalo hunt. (Ibid, 3-4)

The oldest of Samuel I's children was named Nathaniel, who was 15 years old when the family moved to the Blockhouse Bottom. The famous explorer, Daniel Boone, after living in Missouri for several years, moved back to Kentucky and returned to the Big Sandy Valley every winter to hunt bears and sell the hides and bear grease down the river in Cattlettsburg. Boone and his son, Nathan, spent part of the winter of 1796-97 with Samuel's family at Harman's Station, and took young Nathaniel Auxier along on many hunting trips. On these expeditions, Boone and Auxier named several locations for themselves, including Daniel's Creek, Nat's Creek, and Boon's Camp, all of which are still listed as such on maps of the area. One creek was named Greasy Creek because, according to reports (which were probably exaggerated), the hunters packed so much game away from there, the saplings and trees along the trail became greasy from contact with the carcasses and hides of the animals. (AH-ADD3, 15)

Robert Morgan, in his 2008 biography of Daniel Boone, stated that "each winter Daniel and his wife Rebecca and one or two of his sons returned there to kill bears, collect bearskins, smoke bear bacon, and render bear flesh into oil. Bears were so abundant that Boone killed 155 in one season. A bearskin was worth about two dollars, but the meat of each animal was worth more than twice that. Bear grease could be sold for a dollar a gallon. One bear might yield twenty gallons of oil. Boone bragged that he had killed eleven bears before breakfast." (BOONE, 383)

On leaving, Boone presented Samuel one of his long rifles, which he named "Old Smoker," and to Nathaniel a powder horn with the initials "*D. B.*" carved into it. These important relics remained in the possession of Auxier family members for many generations. They were last known to be in the gun collection of Judge Jean Auxier of Pikeville, but alas, the gun and powder horn were given to friends before the Judge passed away. He did not reveal to his family who received the precious heirloom items.

Samuel Auxier II and his wife, Agnes

Boone also gave Samuel's wife, Sarah, a buffalo robe, which she made into a swinging cradle which was attached to the ceiling with leather thongs. (AH – ADD3, 16) This robe was handed down through the generations, and in the 1950's, pieces were trimmed off and distributed to various family members. The largest remaining section, about 18 inches square, was in the possession of Earnest Auxier of Madison, Indiana, until it was lost by a taxidermist who was entrusted to reframe the remaining section of the buffalo robe.

Samuel Auxier II was the next figure in David Valentine's ancestral lineage. This Samuel, sometimes referred to as Virginia Sam, is best remembered for the fact that he raised two large families, and his progeny would eventually number in the thousands. He was married first to Rebecca Phillips, and they had 11 children. Rebecca died on September 20, 1835, and after remaining a widower for a few years, Samuel married Agnes Wells. Five of the six children of this second marriage reached maturity.

Large families were the norm rather than the exception in those days, and for obvious reasons. It was necessary to have lots of "hands" for tending crops, overseeing livestock, procuring game, preparing and preserving food, spinning and weaving cloth, and in the very early days, protecting against

Indian attacks. Virginia Sam was a very successful farmer who continued to oversee his vast interests in his later years astride his favorite horse, Old Suse. (AH, 15)

The children of Virginia Sam and his two wives had large families of their own, and there are many interesting stories therein, but this narrative is about Samuel's grandson, David Valentine Auxier, and thus the focus will remain on his direct line of descendants.

David's father, Nathaniel II, the eldest of Virginia Sam's first family, was born in 1815 in the Blockhouse Bottom. His formal education was average for the community with the exception, as Agnes Auxier wrote, of "one course at Richmond in Madison County, Kentucky." He was an avid reader and was

Nathaniel Auxier

well versed in history, theology, astronomy, politics, and all subjects of common interest. Agnes Auxier wrote in her family history that "Nathaniel was not a public speaker, but he surely had considerable powers of persuasion, whether it was around his own fireside, the hearthstone of a neighbor or relative, or on the public square in Paintsville, the town a few miles downriver." (AH, 22)) Paintsville became the county seat of Johnson County in 1843. Nat was born and died a Democrat and according to Agnes Auxier, named four of his sons after Democrat presidents. They were George Washington, Andrew Jackson, Thomas Jefferson, and James Buchanan.[6] It was said that Nat later became disenchanted with James Buchanan. (AH, 22)

On March 18, 1838, Nathaniel married Hester Ann Mayo in Floyd County, Kentucky. Agnes Auxier had this to say about David Valentine's mother:

---

6 James Buchanan was a Federalist.

"Hester Ann was a thoroughly educated woman, having attended the University of Virginia.7 She came of that stock of Eastern Virginia who believed in thorough education. She was related to John Hancock and also to Frank Mayo, the great actor, who played Davy Crockett and {performed in} many other dramas, comedies, and farces. One of her relatives by the name of Mayo is now a Captain in the U. S. Navy, and being a great writer, furnished many articles for magazines. Another Mayo (Joseph) was mayor of the city of Richmond, and surrendered the city to General Grant on his march to Appomattox. Hester Ann, like her husband, was well informed and a good conversationalist. Thirteen children were the result of this happy union." (AH, 22)

The Mayo name can be traced back to the early 1700's in Virginia. Valentine Mayo's name appears on a deed dated 1702 in Middlesex County, and the given name Valentine is found in the records of Virginia throughout the 1700's and early 1800's. This family tradition accounts for part of the name given David Valentine Auxier, the subject of this book. Hester Ann Mayo's father, Lewis Mayo, was born Feb. 8, 1796 in Fluvanna County, Virginia. (JWC, 530) He received his education in Virginia, married first to Susannah Price, and then to Maria Jones, after which he moved to Floyd and Johnson Counties in Kentucky, and began a long and distinguished teaching career in that region. He died near the end of the Civil War.

David Valentine Auxier was born near the mouth of John's Creek in the Blockhouse Bottom of Johnson County on April 30, 1840. He was the second of thirteen children. Little is

---

7 It is improbable that Hester Mayo attended the University of Virginia. Women of her generation were not admitted to institutions of higher learning, especially in the South.

known of his early life, but his army enlistment records showed his occupation as tanner, a common pursuit in the Auxier family and in the region at that time. He was listed as five feet seven inches tall, with dark complexion, black hair, and black eyes. His letters written during the war, several of which have been preserved, indicate that he was well educated for the time, with a good command of the English language. His mother surely had great influence in that regard, having attended

Captain David Valentine Auxier

school beyond the norm for that period, at least according to family tradition. David apparently became a man of means, stating in his writings that his dream was to use his savings from military service to purchase "good lands in the West." In one of his letters, he indicated that he had sold his interest in a boat store for $1,600.00, a considerable sum in the 1860's, and that he had $700.00 back pay coming.

David was a thinking man, writing philosophically in his letters on matters concerning politics, the war, and slavery. He was against the institution of slavery in all its ramifications and stated so in his correspondence to his cousin Angeline Prater for whom he seemed to have great affection. Angeline, or Ann as she was called, would later become the wife of David's brother, George Washington Auxier. No doubt, David drew much of his ideology about slavery and the war from his father Nathaniel who was outspoken on those subjects. Agnes Auxier wrote that David often accompanied his father to Paintsville and other public gatherings and listened to his impassioned arguments for the maintenance of a perpetual union. Nathaniel had seen as early as 1858 that civil war was brewing and made a decision to stand for the Union. These were the influences surrounding David Valentine as he was formulating his own course of action in the years to come.

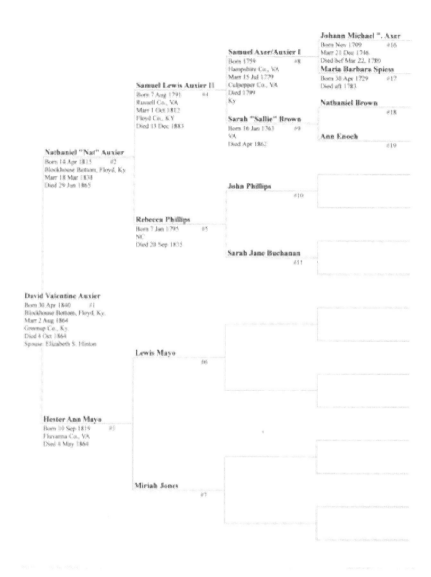

Johann Michael ". Axer
Born Nov 1709   #16
Marr 21 Dec 1746
Died bef Mar 22, 1780

Maria Barbara Spiess
Born 30 Apr 1729   #17
Died aft 1783

Nathaniel Brown
#18

Ann Enoch
#19

Samuel Axer/Auxier I
Born 1754   #8
Hampshire Co., VA
Marr 15 Jul 1779
Culpepper Co., VA
Died 1799
Ky

Sarah "Sallie" Brown
Born 16 Jan 1763   #9
VA,
Died Apr 1862

Samuel Lewis Auxier II
Born 7 Aug 1791   #4
Russell Co., VA
Marr 1 Oct 1812
Floyd Co., KY
Died 13 Dec 1883

John Phillips
#10

Sarah Jane Buchanan
#11

Nathaniel "Nat" Auxier
Born 14 Apr 1815   #2
Blockhouse Bottom, Floyd, Ky
Marr 18 Mar 1838
Died 29 Jun 1865

Rebecca Phillips
Born 7 Jan 1795   #5
NC
Died 20 Sep 1835

David Valentine Auxier
Born 30 Apr 1840   #1
Blockhouse Bottom, Floyd, Ky.
Marr 2 Aug 1864
Greenup Co., Ky.
Died 6 Oct 1864
Spouse: Elizabeth S. Hinton

Lewis Mayo
#6

Hester Ann Mayo
Born 30 Sep 1819   #3
Fluvanna Co., VA
Died 4 May 1864

Miriah Jones
#7

40

BIG
SANDY VALLEY

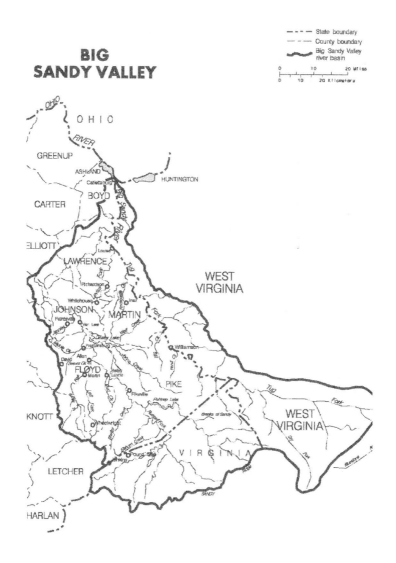

Map Courtesy of John David Preston

BIG
SANDY VALLEY

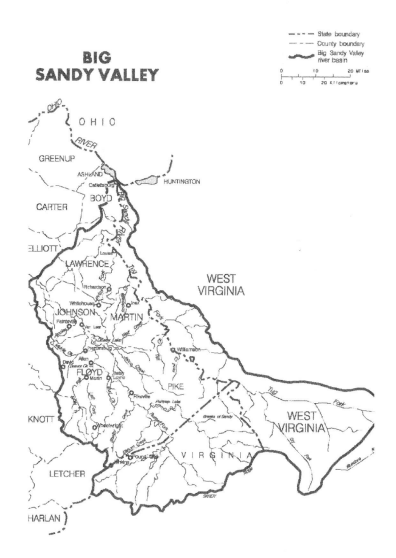

Map Courtesy of John David Preston

CHAPTER IV

REASONS

There was much divergence of political sentiment between the people of the adjacent Floyd and Johnson Counties in the buildup to the Civil War. Most of the leading men of Prestonsburg, the county seat of Floyd County, were on the side of the South and influenced the citizens accordingly. On the other hand, Johnson County took a decided stand for the Northern cause, and later furnished a whole regiment of soldiers for the Union Army. (DVA, 1)A recent book on the history of Johnson County stated that: "... there had been many fights and quarrels around the courthouse in Paintsville as emotions overcame civility." (JCK, 14)

John's Creek, where David's family lived, formed the boundary between Floyd and Johnson Counties, and in spite of the developing split over politics, the two counties

had much in common. The people were alike socially, culturally, and economically, and both counties were about the same size in land area and population. Agriculture was the basis of the economy of the entire region (79% according to the 1860 Kentucky census) and there were very few slaveholders in the four main counties of the Big Sandy Valley. The figure for slaveholders and slaves, respectively, were as follows: Floyd, 40 and 136; Lawrence, 38 and 152; Pike, 28 and 97; and Johnson, 11 and 27. (CW-BSV, 13)

The fact that members of David's extended family owned slaves was surely troublesome to him. David no doubt heard many interesting, and perhaps heated discussions around the family hearths and dinner tables during that time. The slave schedules for Johnson County show that his uncle, John B. Auxier, who was also to become a major influence in David's life, owned one male black under the age of 16 from 1845 to 1850. David's grandfather, Samuel II, owned one male black,

43

age 11 in 1860, and his mother's father, Lewis Mayo, owned three slaves from 1849 to 1860.(KA, 263 -265) Although Samuel II was never active in his political views, when the war broke out, his loyalties remained with the South. One of Sam's younger sons, J. K. Polk Auxier, cast his lot with the Confederacy and served a brief enlistment with the 5th Kentucky Infantry, CSA. "Polk" Auxier also had a nine day enlistment in Company C of the 65th Regiment, Union Army, from May 21, 1864 to May 30, 1864, after which he was reported as a deserter. (JDP, 329) John David Preston wrote that: "One surprising development was the fact that a number of Big Sandy men served on both sides in the conflict. A total of 150 men served in both the Union and Confederate armies. The typical pattern was Confederate service, followed by Union enlistment, although that was not always the case." (CW–BSV, 228)

Another son, Samuel III, known as "Red Sam", also enlisted in the 5th Kentucky Infantry, CSA, and fought in one battle before being discharged for unknown reasons two weeks later. However, according to author, John B. Wells III, Red Sam re-enlisted and was present for duty in the same unit 6 months later.[8] He reportedly owned two slaves, one named Jack who died of consumption in 1855 at the age of 45, and the other was a child, age eleven.

How did David reconcile the fact that certain family members owned slaves at the same time they supported a government that was trying to abolish the very concept and institution of slavery? Did the young man ponder the similarities between his slave-owning family members and Thomas Jefferson, one of the framers of the United States Constitution, himself a slave owner? We can only guess. But it is only fair to remark that many of those who participated in

---

[8] Copy of personal letter from Wells to Judith Need, dated Nov. 6, 1998, in author's possession.

the Civil War did not see it as a war over slavery, but rather over state sovereignty or the preservation of the union

Slavery was not suited to Eastern Kentucky, primarily because the terrain was too rough for large scale farming operations, and also because there was a large available work force.of white farmhands. Additionally, there was no industry large enough to attract workers away from the farms. Roads were almost non-existent in the mid 1800'-s in David Valentine's region of Eastern Kentucky, and indeed,were not essential since there was good river transportation. Most of the commerce was directed north down the Big Sandy toward the Ohio River, rather than west and overland to the so-called bluegrass section of central Kentucky. Most families were pretty much self-sufficient and did not need to travel far from home. During the Civil War, one Union officer estimated that there were not more than 10 wagons between Louisa in Lawrence County, and the Cumberland Mountains at the headwaters of the Big Sandy. (CW–BSV, 16)

In the uneasy times of the late 1850's, Kentucky had struggled to remain neutral in the great conflict. However, when the Confederates invaded Columbus, Kentucky, in September, 1861, the state legislature, prompted by the prevailing Northern point of view in the recent election, requested that the Confederates withdraw from the state. Kentucky could no longer remain neutral in the growing conflict. Regionally, southern sympathizers were elected to represent Floyd and Pike Counties in the state legislature, while Johnson County backed candidates who favored the Union cause. (Ibid, 27)

In October, 1861, Johnson County enacted a resolution banning the display of the flag of either the United States or the Confederate States on the courthouse or the public square. In his book, *The Civil War in the Big Sandy Valley of Kentucky*, John David Preston speculated that the County Court, which was the governing body of Johnson County, was trying to keep the peace between the two factions. They

45

ordered that "... any person or persons who shall put up a flag upon the courthouse or public square representing the United States or the Confederate States, shall by guilty of an offense and shall be fined the sum of $50.00." However, the sentiments locally and regionally were too strong, and loyalties remained divided throughout the war. (CW-BSV, 32)

The resolution apparently had some effect in Johnson County because no fighting units were organized within its boundaries in the ensuing months and years. This is not to say that Johnson County did not furnish large numbers of troops, especially for the Union cause. In fact, most of the men of David Valentine's company, which was formed in the fall of 1862 in neighboring Lawrence County, were from Johnson County. The regiment as a whole was made up of men from Eastern Kentucky, Tennessee, North Carolina, and Virginia, including the region that would become West Virginia after Lincoln's enabling act declared its conditional statehood in 1863. (39th KY)

Presidents Lincoln and Davis,

Generals Grant, and Lee

47

CHAPTER V

TO ARMS

Kentucky was a border state in the Civil War, also known as the War of the Rebellion, the War Between the States, the War of Northern Aggression, and other descriptives, depending on point of view. By 1861, Confederate troops had begun forays into the Big Sandy Valley from Virginia in
efforts to recruit men for the Southern cause. Those efforts were successful in some counties and not at all in those where sentiments were decidedly Unionist.

Col. A. J. May, CSA

The Confederates were the first to organize. Captain Andrew Jackson May of Prestonsburg, formed the 5th Regiment, Infantry, of the Confederacy in October, 1861. The bullets of war first flew in the Big Sandy Valley on November 8, 1861, at Ivy Mountain, about 20 miles downriver from Piketon, which was later renamed Pikeville. A deployment of Union troops from central Kentucky was sent to counteract the activities of the newly organized 5th Infantry. The battle lasted less than four hours, with wildly differing reports of casualties from both sides. The Confederates, with little equipment and virtually no training, were overmatched in the encounter and were soon forced to withdraw their positions overlooking the Big Sandy River. (CW–BSV, 38)   On December 10, 1861, one month after Ivy Mountain, the first local Union regiment, the 14th Kentucky Infantry, was organized at Louisa, just a few miles downriver from Prestonsburg and Paintsville. Col. Laban T. Moore, a former U. S. Congressman from that district, was named commander. (Ibid, 34) Regimental lists showed that by the end of 1861, recruits for the Union 14th Kentucky totaled 550 men, while 435 joined the Confederate 5th Kentucky Infantry. (Ibid, 51)

There was scattered fighting in the region in that first year of the war, with General Humphrey Marshall's Confederate forces marauding up and down the valley from their base in Virginia, and Colonel James A. Garfield's Union troops moving them out, only to have the process repeated.9

Gen. Humphrey Marshall, CSA

Two of the more significant encounters of this period took place on January 10, 1862 at Middle Creek, a tributary of the Big Sandy near Prestonsburg, and on March 16, 1862 at Pound Gap on the Virginia line. David Valentine's enlistment did not occur until September of that year, so I won't go into detail about these conflicts. The point is that fairly serious engagements occurred in the valley. These might have played a role in David Valentine's decision to volunteer, and they certainly created the early context of his military service.

Col. James A. Garfield, USA

Throughout the fall and winter of 1861 and the spring and summer of 1862, the Confederate raids into the Big Sandy Valley escalated, with livestock and crops confiscated, stores robbed, and citizens harassed and in some cases, murdered. The confusion was widespread. An example bearing directly on our present subject was the story of John Dils of Piketon, who was arrested by Confederates in his home in October,

---

9 This is the same James Abram Garfield that later became the 20th president of the United States.

1861, and sent as a P.O.W. to the infamous
Libby Prison in Richmond, Virginia. He was
released a few days before Christmas, but was
accosted and wounded on his way
back to Kentucky. (BSV, 45) In February,
1862, Dils went to Washington to attempt to
relieve himself of any obligation to
serve in the Confederate Army. His memoirs
did not explain why he might be under any
obligation to the Southern cause, but he had
apparently been recruited before his capture
and imprisonment a few months earlier. During his visit to
Washington, he was introduced to President Lincoln who was
impressed by Dils and invited him to visit him at the White
House as often as he could.

Col. John
Dils, USA

  In August, 1862, Dils was robbed at his mercantile store
in Piketon, forcing him to flee to the state capital at Frankfort,
where he met with Sen. J. J. Crittendon and others in an
attempt to procure guns for defense of his property at Piketon.
He got the weapons and a few weeks later received a
commission to recruit a regiment for the U.S. Army in the Big
Sandy Valley. After some self-deliberation, he accepted the
commission and immediately went about the business of
raising the 39th Kentucky Regiment, Mounted Infantry. It was
mustered in on February 16, 1863 with 400 men and 200
more ready to join. Dils was named commander, but was later
dismissed for misappropriation of government property, a
charge which was never fully proven, according to some
historians. (Ibid, 54)

  Other officers of the 39th Kentucky had similar reasons for
joining the ranks of the Union forces in the Valley. Their
primary purpose at that time was to protect the citizenry
against the constant raids being perpetrated upon them by
Southern militia units operating from across the mountains in
Virginia.

  Dr. James H. Hereford of Louisa, Kentucky was contracted
to be Medical Officer for the regiment and served five months

for a fee of $50.00 for the first month and $100.00 for each successive month. (KHS) He was succeeded by Stephen Meek Ferguson who had attended the medical school at Emory and Henry College and like John Dils, had been recruited unsuccessfully by the Confederates. (OM, 1) Ferguson instead joined

Lt. Col. Stephen Meek Ferguson

the 39th Kentucky, with the rank of Major, and was promoted to Lt. Colonel in January, 1864. (Ibid, 6) Henry Scalf's biography of Ferguson notes that his duties in the regiment were not limited to the use of his medical skills but that he also served as Quartermaster. (SMF, 6) By the close of the war, Ferguson was the commanding officer of the 39th Kentucky. His service in the Union Army was made even more complicated because he had two brothers who wore the Confederate gray and yet another one who elected to serve in Union blue. (Ibid, 6)

The 39th Kentucky was originally attached to the District of Eastern Kentucky, Department of the Ohio, but was later assigned to the Department of Kentucky. It was the only three-year regiment that served its entire tour of duty in the mountains of Eastern Kentucky. The regiment did effectively and almost single-handedly protect the region from the bands of roaming thieves and murderers that plagued the mountains during that period. During the war, the regiment lost three officers and twenty-four enlisted men killed and mortally wounded, and three officers and 194 enlisted men by disease, thus a total of 234 did not return from the war. (39th KY)

Other than David Valentine's father, Nathaniel, the man who influenced him most in choosing sides in the war, was his uncle, John Brown Auxier. John B, after the war, was 23 years older than David, and by 1860 had established himself as a highly successful farmer, tanner, miller, and surveyor. In the latter capacity, John B. had surveyed most of the boundaries of Johnson and the adjoining counties, acquiring approximately 10,000 acres of land for fees. 10. John B. also served in the Kentucky State Legislature, representing Floyd and Johnson Counties. The story of how The Major became involved in the war is best told by editor and historian Henry Scalf, in a 1961 article in the *Floyd County Times:*

"It was in this regional spirit of bitterness that John B. Auxier, John's Creek farmer and miller, and a brother of Nathaniel, attended chores at his mill one day. Down the road marched a group of Confederate soldiers, escorting wagon-loads of corn. They demanded he grind it. Auxier, as pro-union as if he had been wearing the Union blue, declared his mill was out of order. The Confederates insisted he must repair it.

Maj. John B. Auxier, USA

Auxier descended to the machinery recessed under the mill floor, pretending to be at work and quietly slipped a stone into the works of the crude turbine. Ascending to the mill proper, he demonstrated to the discomfited rebels that the machinery was inoperative. They took the corn away, muttering in their suspicion of the miller.

A few days later, a friend brought Auxier news. The Confederates had become firmly convinced he had sabotaged his own mill. A Confederate officer was openly vowing to get him.

Auxier decided that it was time for action. He organized a company of men in which two of his nephews, David and George, enlisted. John B. Auxier was named Captain of what was known as Company A,

53

---

10 John B.'s surveying instruments were brought to the 2000 Auxier family reunion at Paintsville, KY, by his great grandson, George A. Auxier of Tennessee

39th Kentucky Volunteer Infantry. John Dils of Pikeville was designated Colonel, commanding. John B. Auxier rose through the military hierarchy to become a Major, and his nephew David succeeded him as Captain. George became a Sergeant." (FCT)

Company A of the 39th Kentucky was officially organized on Nov. 18th, 1862. David Valentine had already enlisted on September 6, 1862 for a period of three years. He was *elected* third lieutenant of Company "A" on November 23, though his certificate, signed by then Governor Beriah Magoffin, mistakenly dated it November 23, *1860*.11 It was the custom at the time for voluntary military units to choose their own leaders. David was twenty-two years old, well educated by local standards, and was a scion of a prominent and well-respected family. It was no surprise that he was chosen for a leadership role. His younger brother, George, was elected a sergeant in Company A by the same process.

Regimental Flag, 39th KY Volunteer Infantry., USA

Even though the 39th Kentucky did not become officially organized until March of 1863, it had already seen action in the Big Sandy Valley. The first significant encounter took place on December 4th, 1862, and was disastrous for the regiment, and for David Valentine and several of his comrades. This was the Battle of Wireman's Shoals, which became known as the Johnson County Boat Fight. The following account is paraphrased from Brian and Hall's CD ROM of the history of the 39th Kentucky Mounted Infantry, US Volunteers:

---

11 See appendix for a copy of David Valentine's third lieutenant certificate.

"In October of 1862, Lt. Levi Hampton, adjutant of the 39th Kentucky, left Pikeville with a detachment of 200 men. He was ordered to procure some push-boats at Peach Orchard in Lawrence County and to continue from there down the Big Sandy River to Catlettsburg, where he would receive some supplies earmarked for

Push boat on the Big Sandy River

the regiment. The trip down the river was uneventful. There were delays in getting the return trip under way and it was not until the last week of November that Lt. Hampton's detachment left Catlettsburg for the trip to Pikeville.

After a week of hard work and due to the low stage of the river, the party reached Wireman's Shoals near the Floyd-Johnson County line on December 3. The Federals encamped on the nearby farm of the father-in-law of one of the hired boatmen.

The Union commander in the region, Col. Jonathan Cranor, had learned from a Union sympathizer that the convoy was in danger of being attacked, and had sent an escort with the boats as far as Peach Orchard. Colonel Dils of the 39th Kentucky, had previously agreed to send an escort to Peach Orchard to accompany the boats for the remainder of their trip to Pikeville. A Cavalry scout reported no Confederate troops in the area, so no escort was sent from the 39th. There were more miscommunications about the eminence of an attack, and when it did come, the boatmen were poorly prepared and were overwhelmed by the 800 Confederate cavalry troops under the command of Col. John N. Clarkson of the Virginia State Line Militia.

The action lasted for no more than an hour. Many of the Federal soldiers surrendered, but quite a few managed to escape to the hills. Official records indicate that the 39th lost one killed and 38 captured. It was also estimated that 10 to 12 Federal soldiers were wounded in the skirmish.

The Confederates also made off with the stores that were being transported on the push-boats. Col. Cranor numbered the losses at 50 to 100 stands of arms, 300 suits of fatigue uniforms, 7,000 rounds of ammunition, a small lot of commissaries, a tent and two push-boats. What Clarkson's men could not carry away, they tried unsuccessfully to destroy. Much of what was left behind by the Confederates was later recaptured. The loss of those supplies had a strong impact on the 39th throughout the winter of 1862-63. The next day, December 5, Companies B and K of the 39th under Col. Dils, would again confront Col. Clarkson's forces at Bull Mountain in Floyd County." (39th KY)

Lt. David Valentine Auxier was among those captured, along with the husband of one of his cousins, Lt. Isaac Goble. "The prisoners were lined up and tied with a long rope knotted around an arm of each. Five guards herded them along one on the front and each side with two in the rear as they marched to Richmond. At night, they were put in rail pens, built from nearby fences, and were fed parched corn. One day they were put to cutting firewood in the forest. An un-named prisoner killed a guard with a stone and escaped. Footsore and ragged, the others finally reached the Richmond prison." (Scalf, DVA, 2)

Isaac Goble, in his application for a military pension in 1882, stated that he, along with David Valentine Auxier and others, was captured at Wireman's Shoals and all were "...marched on foot to a railroad, about 150 miles, thence to Richmond, Va. On the foot march, he was greatly exposed, being compelled to wade streams, and lie in open rail pens at night, then placed in a prison without fire and retained until May, 1863." (USPO-3) Goble went on to claim that the exposure during the march and in the prison caused him to develop rheumatism, which continued to worsen after his discharge on September 15, 1865, severely limiting his ability to do manual labor of any kind. He became a physician after the war.

David Valentine and his group were not treated as official "prisoners of war" because their captors, the Virginia State Line Militia, had not yet aligned with the Confederacy. (CW-BSV, 159) Also, the 39th Kentucky was not full federalized until March of 1863. In short, the official standing of everyone involved was unclear .It should be noted that the penitentiary where the prisoners were held was not the notorious Libby Prison, which was also in Richmond. Contrary to some historians reports that Libby was a tobacco factory, Webb Garrison asserts that it was an unused chandler company owned by "Libby and Sons," which supplied goods and equipment for use onboard ships. (CWH, 134)

David Valentine did not name the prison where he was held, although he did refer to it as a "penitentiary," designed for housing criminals instead of military personnel. The author found a photo of one such prison in Richmond called "Castle Thunder," reportedly named as such because the thunder of cannon could be heard from the premises.

Confederate Prison, Richmond, VA

CHAPTER VI

PRISON

David Valentine apparently wrote several letters to his father while confined in the prison in Richmond, but the only one that has been preserved by family members is dated April 7, 1863. 12   In it, he described his apparent good health despite the wretched conditions where he and his comrades were being held, and he asks his father to intercede for him and his fellow inmates:

"Penitentiary, Richmond, Va., April 7th, 1863

Mr. Nathaniel Auxier, Paintsville, Johnson Co. Ky.
My Dear Father and Mother,

I have once more the opportunity of writing to you, but I do not know whether this will ever reach you or not. I am well as to health but I long to be out of this wretched place to enjoy once more the pure fresh air and feel myself again a free man. I have been locked up in this wretched penitentiary ever since the 30th of December and I have no idea when I will be released. I wrote you a short letter soon after I came here stating where I am, etc. I also wrote to Colonel J. Dils giving him the particulars of how we are being held. It seems that our govt. holds a prisoner who bears the appellation Col. Zarvona, alias Col. Thomas, who was captured soon after the war broke out, and said Zarvona or Thomas, bears a commission from Governor Letcher, on account of which he cannot be exchanged under the cartel. We being captured by the

59

---

12 See appendix for reproductions of some of David Valentine's original letters.

Va. State Line troops, places us in the same situation. The Governor, therefore, ordered that Capt. Thomas Damron, Lieut. Wilson Damron, Lieut. Isaac Goble and myself, and J. W. Mims, Wm. S. Dils, and Samuel Pack, be held in close confinement in the penitentiary until our gov't agrees to release Col. Thomas. I want you to write to me immediately on the receipt of this, and if you think you can do anything to effect an exchange for us, I want you to do it. There are seven of us and we will pay any expense that you may incur for us. If there is any chance that you can do anything, do it (even) if it is to go to Washington City. We think that if we had a good friend there, that our release could be brought about. Get recommendations from Cranor, L. T. Moore, and others of influence.

Tell Colonel Dils to retain Isaac Goble's and my commissions, and tell Capt. Auxier to draw and receipt for our wages and hand it over to you, and Isaac wants you to let his wife have his part of it. If you undertake to do anything for us, retain money enough to pay yourself out of it. If you go to Washington, Damron requests you to get John Richson to go with you. I must now close, my paper gives out. Good bye. I hope I will get home some day.
I remain your obedient son.   David V. Auxier"

The "cartel" referred to in David's letter between the Union and Confederacy had been in effect only a few months when he and his comrades were placed in the prison in Richmond. The following essay, written by Stephen T. Foster, a member of the Memphis Metal Detector Club in 1995, outlines clearly and succinctly the history and scope of the program:

"At the start of the Civil War, a formal exchange system for prisoners of was not arranged because

President Lincoln did not recognize the Confederacy as having wartime rights. However, after the defeat of Union forces at the 1st Battle of Bull Run, with a large number of Union prisoners held by the Confederacy, the U. S. Congress requested that Lincoln take measures to effect an exchange. Up to this time, opposing commanders would sometimes arrange an exchange of their prisoners under a flag of truce, but these transactions were few.

The first government-sanctioned exchanges took place in February, 1862, but it was not until July 22 that a formal cartel detailing the exchange system was agreed to by the two governments. Under this agreement, all prisoners were to be released, either by exchange or parole, within 10 days of capture. An equivalency table was devised in which a certain number of enlisted men could be exchanged for an officer. (Footnote with equivalency table: 1 General = 46 Privates, 1 Major General = 40 Privates, 1 Brigadier General = 20 Privates, 1 Colonel = 15 Privates, 1 Lt. Colonel = 10 Privates, 1 Major = 8 Privates, 1 Captain = 6 Privates, 1 Lieutenant = 4 Privates, 1 Noncommissioned Officer = 2 Privates) Excess prisoners who could not be exchanged were to be released on parole, which meant they could not perform any military service until they were officially notified that they had been exchanged.

The system was bogged down by paperwork, and each side found reason to interrupt exchanges from time to time. The cartel operated reasonably well until it broke down in the summer of 1863. By that time, the Federal government had begun to use black soldiers in its war effort. Refusing to recognize captured blacks as prisoners of war, the Confederacy reduced them to slave status and threatened to execute as insurrectionists the Union officers who had commanded them. A retaliatory threat by the Union prevented the Confederacy from carrying out any executions, but did not restore the cartel. Several times later in the war, the Southern states needed soldiers and requested that the exchanges resume, but Gen Ulysses S. Grant, with plenty of Union soldiers, refused." (Foster)

Within a week after David Valentine and his fellow prisoners were confined in the penitentiary in Richmond, they were told by prison officials that they were being held in retaliation for the confinement of a Colonel Zarvona who had been captured by Union forces and was being held in a Northern prison. David Valentine's group started a letter-writing campaign in an attempt to gain their freedom through the cartel. They proposed a swap of their group of four officers and three enlisted men for this Col. Zarvona, whose real name was Richard Thomas. The following is a letter to Secretary of War Edwin M. Stanton, from David Valentine, Lieut. Isaac Goble, and John W. Howe:

"Penitentiary, Richmond, Va., Jan. 5, 1863

Mr. Stanton, Secretary of War,

Edwin M. Stanton, Sec. of War

Sir: We are prisoners of war held by the State of Virginia and we are confined in the State Penitentiary as a means of retaliation for the confinement of one Colonel Zarvona and others held by the Government of the United States. Said Zarvona bears a commission from the State of Virginia and is said to be in confinement in some of our Northern prisons. We were taken prisoners in Floyd County, Ky, by Maj. Gen. John B. Floyd, commanding State troops. We were handed over to Governor Letcher, who issued an order confining us to solitary confinement in the State Penitentiary until we were exchanged for Colonel Zarvona and others. We therefore beseech you to effect an exchange for us as soon as possible. A copy of the Governor's order has been forwarded to you already.

Very sincerely yours,

David V. Auxier, Isaac Goble, John W. Howe" (OR, Series II, Vol. 5, p. 223)

Who was this "Zarvona," alias Richard Thomas fellow? It is an interesting story which will be detailed at length in the following chapter. On February 5, David wrote to his U.S. Representative, the Honorable G. W. Dunlap to ask for his assistance in obtaining an exchange.

"Penitentiary of Virginia, Richmond, February 5, 1863

Hon. G. W. Dunlap,

Sir: Your petitioners are prisoners of war confined in the penitentiary of this city. We are held as hostages for one Colonel Thomas, who we understand is confined in Baltimore or some other place. We have been prisoners more than three months, one half of which has been in this loathsome place where we have suffered extremely. We were brought to this place on the 31st of December last, since which time we have been kept in close confinement. Our rooms are very small and of course not very comfortable. Our diet is the same as the convicts. We were captured by Gen. John B. Floyd, commanding the Virginia State Line, in consequence of which we are deprived of the cartel for the exchange of prisoners between the two governments. There are seven of us held for the release of one man. We should think our Government ought to make the exchange without hesitation. It would certainly be to their advantage to get seven men in place of one. There are four officers among us and very gallant ones, too, at that, viz, Captain Damron of Western Virginia State Guards; Lieutenant Damron of Western Virginia State Guards; Isaac Goble, First Lieutenant, 39th Regiment, Kentucky Volunteers; David V. Auxier, second lieutenant, 39th Regiment, Kentucky Volunteers. The privates are Samuel Pack, Virginia State Guards; William S. Dils, Lawrence County, Ohio, and John W. Howe, Johnson County, Ky.

We have written several letters to Secretary Stanton upon the subject but have received no reply; we therefore concluded to write to you as our representative, imploring you to aid us in our present suffering condition. The whole matter is at the discretion of our Government. Governor Letcher has long since notified our government of his readiness to exchange us.

Capt. Thomas Damron, W. S. Dils and S. Pack request that you show this letter to Hon. Kellian V. Whaley, of Virginia, for perusal, request that he aid you in our release. Please write to my father, Nathaniel Auxier, Johnson County, Penceville (Paintsville) Post Office, Ky., and acquaint him of my situation and you will greatly oblige his son David V. Auxier. Please write us as soon as possible and let us know whether we will be exchanged or not. Very respectfully, your obedient servants,

David V. Auxier, Isaac Goble, J. S. Howe, W. S. Dils, Samuel Pack, Thomas Damron, Wilson Damron" (OR, Series II, Vol II, p. 407)

CHAPTER VII

ZARVONA – THE FRENCH LADY

There are no less than 95 listings of correspondence in the *Record of the War of the Rebellion* concerning this interesting fellow, including five mentioning David Valentine Auxier by name. There are letters to President Lincoln, General G. B. McClellan, Virginia Governor John Letcher, Richmond Mayor Joseph Mayo, Secretary of State William H. Seward, Secretary of the Interior Caleb B. Smith, and various other Adjutant Generals, Under-Secretaries, and government officials. A lengthy letter from Governor Letcher to President Lincoln, dated January 2, 1863, outlined the Governor's view of the terms of the cartel. He went into great detail about Colonel Zarvona and the conditions of his capture and imprisonment, first in Fort McHenry, and later in Fort Lafayette. Letcher wrote that "Zarvona was being confined as a felon in a dungeon, and subjected to the greatest inhumanity." (OR, Series II, Vol. 2, p. 401) Governor Letcher explained that Zarvona has been held in close confinement for eighteen months and that not one of the provisions contained in the cartel has been complied with. (Ibid, 402) In the closing paragraph, Letcher mentioned by name the seven Union officers and men, including David Valentine Auxier, who would be held in the prison in Richmond until an exchange for Zarvona could be agreed upon. (Ibid, 403)

Governor Letcher had more than a passing interest in the case of Zarvona, his militia colonel, to whom he had given a commission in the Virginia Volunteers, dated July 1, 1861. (Ibid, 380). Thomas, who only later went by Zarvona, had written to Letcher on April 26, asking for a commission as an engineer or topographical engineer, or staff, or anything else related to naval warfare. He declares that he would like to "avoid the fatigues of a private's life, which I admit I am little prepared for." In the letter, he outlined in great detail his ideas about how he could take a small, armed gunboat and commandeer Union steamers operating around the coast of Maryland. Thomas boasted that he could easily raise 150 men if the governor would furnish cannons, carbines, cutlasses, and knives to outfit vessels under the Confederate flag. (Ibid, 400)

Later, after Thomas (Zarvona) was captured and confined in a Union prison, Letcher wrote a lengthy letter to President Lincoln, stating that Zarvona was acting under specific orders from the sovereign State of Virginia, and that Zarvona should be treated as a *prisoner of war* and not as a felon held in a dungeon and subjected to the greatest inhumanity. Letcher further entreated the President to issue orders making Zarvona eligible for the exchange cartel. (Ibid, 401)

The Zarvona story is outlined in some detail in a magazine article published in *The Civil War Times*, May/June 1992, by John D. and Linda C. Pelzer. It was entitled, *"Zarvona, the French Lady,"* and the sidebar said "The Confederates needed an adventurer with a flair for the unusual to play the lead role in an undercover operation to capture a Federal gunboat." Richard Thomas "Zarvona" was their man (or lady). The nephew of a former Maryland governor and son of a president of the state senate, he enrolled at West Point but chafed under the regimented lifestyle of the cadets. Thomas struck out on a series of jobs and adventures as a government surveyor, a mercenary battling revolutionaries in China, and later fighting pirates in Italy. It was in this latter endeavor that he assumed the name "Zarvona." (CWT, 29)

In September, 1860, the Union Navy launched its newest and most powerful warship in the Potomac flotilla, the *"Pawnee."* George Hollins, a Confederate Naval Commander (and former United States Navy Officer), concocted a plan to capture the Pawnee for use in the virtually non-existent Confederate Navy.(Ibid, 30)

Commander George Hollins, CSA

Zarvona entered the picture when Governor Letcher, an enthusiastic supporter of the plot, introduced him to George Hollins of Maryland. Hollins was taken by Zarvona's zest for the dangerous mission, and the two of them fleshed out the details of the action. It would entail capturing a small passenger boat, the "St. Nicholas," which regularly had close contact with the Pawnee through delivery of mail and supplies to the warship. (Ibid, 29-30)

The first step was successfully accomplished on June 28, 1861, when 25 soldiers of the Zarvona task force, all dressed in workmen's clothes, and each carrying a toolbox containing concealed weapons, boarded the St. Nicholas at Baltimore. They were not a conspicuous group, primarily because of Zarvona's masterful distraction in his performance as the French Lady. He wore a woman's hoop skirt and carried all the accessories of a flirtatious young French mademoiselle. Confederates on board later recalled that he "tossed his fan around and put on the airs of an animated French Lady." (Ibid, p. 30)

The "French Lady"
(From *The Civil War Times Illustrated*, May/June, 1992)

George Hollins boarded at the next port of call, and soon after, the pirates broke out their weapons and commandeered the vessel. Hollins ordered the captain to head for the Virginia shore where they were joined by members of a regiment of Confederates from Tennessee. To their disappointment, the party learned that the Pawnee was safely moored at the Washington Navy Yard, necessitating a change of plans. Hollins ordered the Captain of the St. Nicholas to head up the Rappahannock River toward Fredericksburg. On their way, they encountered and captured three brigs and schooners with their valuable cargos of coffee, ice, and coal. (Ibid, 31)

The daring capture of the St. Nicholas and the other three vessels made heroes of the group in the Southern press, with promotions for the leaders of the operation. Zarvona garnered most of the public attention, and he decided he wanted another shot at the limelight. In an attempt to duplicate his earlier success, he was recognized when he boarded yet another boat. After a 90-minute search, the "French Lady" was discovered concealed in the drawer of a bureau in the ladies cabin, in the aft part of the boat. Zarvona and his four co-conspirators were taken into custody at Ft. McHenry in Maryland where Zarvona was imprisoned and later transferred to Fort Lafayette in New York Harbor. (CWH, 34) His health deteriorated while in prison and he attempted to escape several times, coming closest to success on the night of April 21, 1862, when he scaled the fort wall and swam across the harbor before being recaptured. (CWT, 67)

Dozens of letters were exchanged about the efforts of Zarvona and others on his behalf, to obtain his release, all of which came to naught, with the main justification citing the prisoner's intent to do harm to the property and personnel of the Federal government, and also his propensity for attempting to escape confinement. In a letter dated Sept. 10, 1861 from Major General John A. Dix, Commander of Fort Monroe to Major General G. B. McClellan, Dix said,

> "One (of our prisoners) is the celebrated Thomas or Colonel Zarvona, commonly known as the French lady. He is one of the first families in Maryland; is rich, intelligent and resolute. His nervous system is much broken by confinement and want of active occupation and he has made earnest appeals to me for the privilege of walking about the garrison within the walls on his parole of honor not to attempt to escape. There is no doubt it would be sacredly respected. I have not

thought proper to extend the indulgence to him, though I think his health requires it, without your direction." OR, Series II, Vol. 2, p. 381)

McClellan's response was that he did not think it prudent to extend his liberty. (Ibid, 381)

A year later, General Dix added this assessment in a letter to Brigadier. General L. Thomas, Adjutant-General, U.S. Army:

> "In regard to Zarvona, please say to the Secretary of War that he is a crack-brained fellow who can do no mischief beyond his individual capacity, mental and physical, which is constitutionally small." (Ibid, 401)

A resolution adopted by the U. S. Senate on January 28, 1863, states as follows:
> "Resolved, That the Committee on Military Affairs and the Militia be instructed to inquire for the purpose of extending such relief as the circumstances may require into the case of Mr. Thomas [Zarvona] of Maryland, now a prisoner of war at Fort Lafayette, who it is represented has been confined in a dungeon at that fortress since June last and is now hopelessly insane by reason of his sufferings." (Ibid, 403)

Conversely, a report from a Dr. W. H. Studley, Acting Assistant Surgeon at Fort Lafayette, dated February 2, 1863, stated that he had examined Colonel Richard Thomas Zarvona and found him to be "in generally good health, social, rational, but somewhat eccentric." The doctor deemed his peculiarities perfectly consistent with sanity of mind. (Ibid, pp. 405-406)

Zarvona was eventually transferred to Fort Delaware in April, 1863, and exchanged for David Valentine Auxier and three other Union officers and three privates. His freedom was conditioned upon leaving the country and refraining from war action. He kept his word and left the United States to live the rest of his life in France. (CWT, 67)

On May 2, 1863, Robert Ould, Agent for Exchange of Prisoners for the Confederate States of America, wrote to the Hon. James A. Seddon, Secretary of War, CSA, recommending that a sufficient number of Federal officers now being held be set aside to retaliate for "the unjust detention of the following named person (Zarvona)." (OR, Series II, Vol. 2, p. 414). A response from a representative of Governor Letcher stated on May 16 that:

> "I have the honor to state that on the 6th instant the governor transmitted to the superintendent the following paper": 'Hostages for Colonel Zarvona: Capt. Thomas Damron, Lieut. Wilson Damron, Lieut. David V. Auxier, Lieut. Isaac Goble, Privates Samuel Pack, William S. Dils, J. W. Howe. Colonel Bass will at once release the prisoners named herein and hand them over to the Confederate authorities for exchange for Zarvona. John Letcher'" (Ibid, p 14)

On May 17, a Captain Thomas P. Turner of the Confederate prison in Richmond endorsed the exchange as follows:
> "The within-mentioned officers were paroled May 5, 1863. They were paroled and sent home by flag of truce May 15, 1863, as citizen prisoners. They were captured in Floyd County, Ky., Dec. 4, 1862." (Ibid, 415).

David Valentine was paroled at City Point, VA, on May 5, 1863, reported at Camp Parole, MD., on May 7, and was ordered to report to his regiment on May 8, 1863. (POW) We have no record of David Valentine's return to Kentucky, presumably on foot, through enemy lines, bearing a flag of truce for protection. We may assume that it was hazardous. Henry Scalf wrote in his monograph that one of David's comrades, James Y. Brown, was ill and collapsed on the way. Brown's sons rode horse back to bring their father back from a Maryland farmhouse to the Big Sandy Valley. (DVA, 3)

When David finally arrived back home in Kentucky, he found that many things were not well in his family. His mother, Hester, was ill and died the following year.13 His father, Nathaniel, who so longed to see his America a united country, did not live to see Lee's surrender. He died January 24, 1865. (DVA, 3) With David Valentine and George Washington still in service, younger brother Andrew Jackson Auxier, temporarily became the family head. Andrew later became a famous jurist in the Big Sandy Valley.

It goes without saying that when David Valentine enlisted in the 39th Kentucky Volunteer Infantry, he did not envision spending the first six months of his tour of duty in a Confederate prison. Nor is it likely that he foresaw the fact that he and several of his *compadres* would be held as pawns in exchange for a southern militia officer. Furthermore, it would have seemed improbable that after the war, the whole Zarvona story would be chronicled in the massive 126 volume *Record of the War of the Rebellion* and that Captain David Valentine Auxier's name would be mentioned prominently in a substantial number of the entries in that series.

13 Hester Mayo Auxier died May 4, 1864.

CHAPTER VIII

RETURN TO ACTION

The Record of the War of the Rebellion is replete with accounts of the activities and accomplishments of the 39th Kentucky Volunteer Mounted Infantry regiment. One such report mentions Major John B. Auxier, one of the regimental commanders, who "traveled 55 miles in less than 24 hours over a country with scarcely any roads." His mission was to support the main contingent of the 39th Kentucky in pursuit of a rebel detachment under the command of a Colonel Prentice.(OR, Series I, Vol. 32, p. 648).

When David Valentine returned to his unit in Eastern Kentucky in June, 1863, he found that the 39th Kentucky would soon be involved in a steady string of small skirmishes up and down the Big Sandy Valley. Some of the locations had colorful names like Bull's Gap, Mouth of Coal Run, Pond Creek, Cracker's Neck, Beaver Creek, Clark's Neck, Marrowbone Creek, Brushy Creek, Half Mountain, and Puncheon.

Rarely during this period did his regiment venture over the state line into West Virginia. On one of these occasions, the 39th KY joined forces with its sister cavalry units, the 10th KY and the 14th KY, along with several others from Ohio and Illinois, to attack an enemy force at Gladesville, WV. Brigadier General Julius White, commander of the Eastern Kentucky Federals, gave this report on July 11, 1863:

> "This command (of about 950 men) reached Gladesville after some skirmishing along the way, completely surprising and carrying the place by storm, beating in the doors and windows from which the enemy were firing, with axes, and compelling his surrender after fifteen minutes of close and desperate fighting, during which the loss of the enemy was 20

73

killed and 30 wounded. Eighteen commissioned officers, including Colonel Caudill, commanding the regiment, were surrendered, with 99 enlisted men. The camp equipage, stores, arms, and ammunition of the command were destroyed." (Ibid, 819-820)

David Valentine mentioned this battle in a letter to his cousin Angeline Prater, dated July 16, 1863. After some felicitations and a report that he was in good health, he wrote:

"I have been over in Logan Co., WV. We captured about 30 prisoners while the 10th KY Cavalry and 1st Company Squadron went to Glade Mill and captured Col. Caudill and 127 of his men. I do not think the war can last a great while longer. We have Vicksburg, Ten. [sic]. Lee is whipped and everything seems to be working favorable for us and I hope the war will soon end. But I am not tired of the service and under no conditions would I leave the service until the end of the war. I believe that I am fighting a holy and just cause and that God, who presides in the destiny of nations, will defend the right and restore the Union."

Angeline was David Valentine's double first cousin. She lived on Burning Fork of the Licking River near Salyersville in Magoffin County, about 20 miles from David's home in Johnson County. This letter to Angeline was the first of three after his release from the prison in Richmond. He seemed to have a measure of affection for Angeline as revealed in his other letters to her. He closed one note to her with: "Write to me the first chance you have. Give my love to all and reserve a good portion of it for yourself."

Angeline later married David Valentine's younger brother George on Dec. 3, 1865, her birthday. She was a woman of great spirit, as revealed in this account in an addendum to Agnes Auxier's 1908 history and genealogy of the Auxier family:

"When she (Angeline) was a girl of twenty, (John Hunt) Morgan's men (the famous "Morgan's Raiders") came down Burning Fork, Magoffin County, to her father's home, where they thought he had hidden his neighbor and kinsman, Reuben Patrick. (Patrick was a daring scout for the Union Army). Believing Angeline's father was lying when he told them he knew nothing of Patrick's whereabouts, they lined him up to be shot. Ann threw herself in front of her father, telling the soldiers they would have to kill her first. They admired her bravery so much they spared her father's life but camped nearby, killed their chickens, hogs and cattle, cooked them in their big wash kettles, and ate them before their eyes." (AH–ADD-1, p. 3)

Angeline
Prater
Auxier

In a March 1, 1864 letter to his father Nathaniel, David Valentine wrote about the progress of the war from his perspective:

"Dear Papa, I have just returned from Louisville where I have been with prisoners. There is not a great deal of news. General Sherman is advancing into Alabama. He has taken Selma and now threatens Mobile. The cars and boats are full of soldiers going to the front, and coming home on furlough. There will soon be a good deal of activity in all the armies.

I learn, since I have come back, that I have been recommended for the Captaincy of Company A. I don't know that such is positively the case, but believe it is. I do not know when I will get to come home, maybe not this spring. I rather believe that Kentucky will be invaded at some point as there is no other place except this, we may look for the Rebels down Sandy or from this part of Virginia. There is not over 6,000 of our cavalry at Mt. Sterling and in a short time there will be at least 20,000. So you may guess what you please. I do not think this report ought have been circulated, but it seems that no move can be made without the knowledge of everybody.

The proceedings of the Louisville convention will be furnished you before long for circulation. It is very interesting, and I hope that the people of Kentucky will adopt some speedy measures for the emancipation of her slaves, and I am not very particular what they are.

I am respectfully your son, D. V. Auxier."

President Lincoln had issued a "preliminary Emancipation Proclamation" in September, 1862, preparing the nation for the final edict, which took effect on January 1, 1863. But this proclamation applied only to states in open rebellion against the United States of America, and that did not include the states of Delaware, Maryland, Kentucky and Missouri, in which slavery was legal, but secession had not been consummated (although it was certainly tried in both Kentucky and Missouri). Thus, slave states still within the union were encouraged to emancipate the slaves in the most expedient way that would be consistent with their self government. Kentuckians as a whole had not supported Lincoln or the Republican administration on the subject of freeing the slaves, and had in fact protested (sometimes violently) all efforts to abolish slavery. Even after December 18, 1865 when the 13th Amendment *officially* ended the institution of slavery in the United States, the people of Kentucky rejected the idea and the commonwealth did not officially adopt the amendment until 1976. (FILSON)

Kentucky's dissatisfaction with Lincoln and his administration intensified once the federal army began enlisting black soldiers. Realizing the delicate situation in

Kentucky, Lincoln initially exempted the state from black enlistment. However, by March 1864, recruiting stations had opened across the state and many slaves and free blacks flocked to join. (Ibid)

In the Spring of 1864, presumably soon after David Valentine's March 1 letter to his father, a detachment from the 39th Kentucky under the command of now *Captain* David Valentine Auxier, was sent to Greenupsburg – later renamed Greenup - on the Ohio River. This detachment, consisting of about 45 men, was assigned to recruit troops for the U. S. Army, particularly from the colored population. There is no record that the 39th KY had colored soldiers, but regiments of colored soldiers were being assembled in some of the northern states. The 5th Colored Infantry which would later serve heroically in the Battle of Saltville, Virginia, was being formed in Central Kentucky.

David Valentine's younger brother, George, was at that time a private in David's company, and was assigned to accompany the Greenupsburg mission. George was one of several men who performed quartermaster duty, making trips into the surrounding farming country to purchase forage for the horses and suitable food for the soldiers. Some of the men became ill and were not able to eat the government issued rations. According to affidavits in George's pension applications after the war, the sick troops would swap rations to the farmers for fresh vegetables and meats which were more palatable for their queasy stomachs. (USPO-3, 4) It was on one of these food and forage gathering excursions that George suffered a broken leg, which would cause him much pain and misery for the remainder of his life. He and another soldier were riding in a buckboard pulled by one horse when a child dashed out in front of the horse, causing it to kick through a board on the front of the wagon, striking George on the right leg just below the knee. It was an ugly fracture with pieces of bone protruding through the skin. The detachment being small, had no medical officer with it, so George was taken to a private physician in the county seat of Greenupsburg. The doctor set the leg the best he was able and treated him in his clinic for a period of time. (Ibid)

The wound never healed due to infection and drainage, even after subsequent treatment by army doctors and private physicians. In his application for a military pension in the 1880's, George tried unsuccessfully to connect his chronic rheumatism to the broken leg, but the adjutant general ruled that the affliction was not service connected. Unfortunately, George's companion in the wagon at the time of the accident could not remember if the injury was received while they were on duty. (Ibid)

George returned to duty after a brief recuperation and persevered for the remainder of the war despite his bad leg. Dozens of his fellow soldiers, and later many of his friends, family, and neighbors, swore under oath that the leg severely hampered his ability to do any kind of manual labor. It was reported that George sometimes cried out in pain when being helped on his horse throughout his adult life. (Ibid)

The lameness and/or rheumatism did not prevent George from marrying and raising a family. After the war, he married Angeline Prater, the cousin with whom David Valentine corresponded for a period of time. As I detailed in chapter two, George became a productive and prominent citizen in Johnson County.

It is unclear when David Valentine's tour of duty in Greenup County ended, but during that period, he met and married a seventeen year old girl named Elizabeth Hinton, or "Lizzie," as he called her in his letters to his father and to his cousin Angeline Prater. In an August 29, 1864 letter to Angeline, he wrote:

> "I have nothing of special interest to write you, only I am no longer a single man. I have been married ever since the 2nd of August. I have the dearest wife you ever saw, but Aunt Mary will tell you all about her."

This letter was written from Mt. Sterling, Kentucky, where a large number of troops were being assembled for campaigns against a possible invasion of the state by Confederate General John Hunt Morgan's Raiders, and for the as-yet unannounced attack on the strategically important salt works just over the state line in Virginia.

In another letter to his father from the camp at Mt. Sterling, David Valentine wrote:

"Lizzie is here with me. I wrote to you some time ago in regard to our marriage. When we were married, her father was very sick, and he died in a week after we were married. She now has no father or mother. She is a very sensible good girl, and I think you will like her very much. She has $300.00 in gold which is now worth $750.00 in greenbacks. She wants it invested in a good farm somewhere. At the death of her father, I was appointed guardian for her little brother John, and I have $100.00 in gold which belongs to him on which I am to pay six percent interest until he is of age. He is now 12 years old.

CHAPTER IX

SALTVILLE

The presence of salt in the underground waters on the border between Smyth and Washington Counties in southwest Virginia had been known since the 1750's. (SWV-CW, Ac). An unincorporated town, soon to be called "Saltville," sprung up to develop the industry of distilling the saline water into the white crystalline substance which was so important for seasoning and preserving food. Little did the locals know how important their commodity would become in the war. "No military force could move without horses, which required heavy doses of salt, and every article of leather from shoes to cartridge belts to harness came from the hides initially treated by salt. Most important, though, was the consideration that both the civilian and military population subsisted on a diet of pork, bacon, and beef preserved in either salt or brine." (Ibid, 14)   By 1859, the salt works, owned by a man named Thomas L. Preston, was not doing well, prompting him to lease his interests to entrepreneurs from Syracuse, New York. However, the Preston family retained ownership of the land itself, a fortuitous move, and the Preston family attained great wealth in the ensuing years, with many of them becoming prominent in the law and education professions. (Ibid, Ad).   In 1860, Washington County was the home of Confederate Secretary of War John B. Floyd, and its county seat, Abingdon, attracted many prominent lawyers and jurists. Emory and Henry College had been growing since it was established in 1836, and the area began a period of economic prosperity and educational prominence.   By the late spring and early summer of 1864, General Stephen Gano Burbridge, military governor of Kentucky, had designs on the salt works just over the line and was assembling a large force of soldiers at Mt. Sterling, estimated to be 6,000 to 8,000 in number, but was distracted from that objective when Confederate General John

Hunt Morgan, a native Kentuckian, captured Mt. Sterling on June 9th. Morgan was subsequently defeated in a battle at Cynthiana on June 12th. David Valentine's unit fought in both of these severe engagements. The 39th KY Mounted Infantry lost 4 men killed and a half dozen others wounded (CW – BSV, p. 208) David's uncle, Major John B. Auxier, was wounded by a sword to the cheek Burbridge pursued Morgan with 6,000 men, but ran out of supplies and was not able to catch him before he escaped back to Virginia with, by his account, two thousand seven hundred prisoners and a large number of (loaded) wagons." (W-SWV, p. 110) These engagements and their aftermath only delayed Burbridge's plans for a march to Southwest Virginia.

Gen. John Hunt Morgan, CSA

There were five principal sources of salt in the South, and Saltville had the largest reservoir of any of the five locations. The Saltville pots kept boiling almost non-stop during the war, producing thousands of bushels on a daily basis. (SWV-CW, 14) "As many as 2,600 kettles seethed in the kilns, and a Yankee observer later guessed there were three hundred buildings associated with the various works." (Ibid, 99)

As strategic as the supply of salt was to the Confederacy, the salt works were poorly defended and vulnerable to attack. By 1862, there were fewer than 2,000 men available to guard the border between Southwestern Virginia and Eastern Kentucky, and they were poorly trained, poorly organized, and poorly equipped. Governor Letcher of Virginia authorized the organization of a State Line Militia for all of western Virginia, with John Floyd as its commander with the rank of Major General. (Ibid, 22) Elements of Colonel Floyd's militia were responsible for the surprise attack on the Union flotilla at Wireman's Shoals on the Big Sandy River in December of 1862. This was the action in which David Valentine Auxier was captured and taken to a prison in Richmond, Virginia.

This militia unit was not officially aligned with the Confederacy at that point. Burbridge was 32 years old and had been breveted Major General after his repulse of John Hunt Morgan. He was reported to have owned "scores of slaves." He was unpopular with many people, not the least of which was Morgan himself. After the battle, Morgan wrote the following letter:

> Brig. Gen. S. G. Burbridge, Commanding U. S. Forces in Kentucky:
>
> GENERAL: Information has reached me that General Hobson and staff, who were captured "Abingdon, July 17, 1864.
> by the forces under my command at Cynthiana, Ky., on the 11th ultimo [June], have been returned to duty, and that the officers who were deputed by me to accompany them to Cincinnati under flag of truce have been retained as prisoners of war. I am very loath to believe that all this is true, the more so since it was at the earnest solicitation of General Hobson himself that he was permitted to return within your lines. He gave his parole of honor that if he was not successful in his efforts to exchange himself and staff for officers of my command now held by the Federal Government that he would return with the flag within my lines wherever they might be at the time this result was determined. It has been some five weeks since the flag referred to was sent out and yet nothing has been heard from it. I cannot think there has been so flagrant a violation of faith as is herein indicated, and to promote a better understanding I beg leave respectfully to ask what has been the action of your Government in the premises.
> I am, very respectfully, & c.
>   Jno. H. Morgan,
>   Brigadier General, Commanding"
> (OR, Series II, vol. VII, p. 469)

After Burbridge learned of Morgan's death in an ambush in Greeneville, Tennessee in September, he returned his attention to Saltville. He wanted desperately to revenge his humiliating defeat by Morgan at Mt. Sterling and Lexington. (SWV - CW, p.100)

The South knew that Burbridge was planning an attack on the salt works, but many of the Union generals, including General William T. Sherman, were not of the opinion that a push on Southwest Virginia "was the best course at this time." Sherman wrote to Major General John M. Schofield: "I doubt the necessity of your sending far into Virginia to destroy the salt work, or any material interest, we must destroy their armies." (Ibid, 113)

Gen. Stephen G. Burbridge, USA

Gary C. Walker wrote that when Burbridge started out of Kentucky toward Saltville, he was:

> "...easily the most roundly despised man in the state of Kentucky. The people hated him because of the heavy handed tactics he used as military governor. Harsh reprisals were inflicted on the civilians because of Confederate guerrilla activity, and he forced the people to sell their produce below a fair market value to the government. He even ordered the arrest of anyone suspected of opposing the re-election of Abraham Lincoln." (Ibid, 115)

Burbridge was not in good graces with some of his military superiors, including General Sherman because he had ordered the recruitment of colored soldiers in Kentucky. Most of these were freed slaves who were thought to be not the best material for a well-trained and disciplined fighting force.

Burbridge had 12 regimental units under his command, a total of 5,200 men. Included in the aggregation were David Valentine's 39th Kentucky Mounted Cavalry and other regiments from Kentucky, Ohio, and Michigan, along with the newly formed 5th U. S. Colored Cavalry. The "coloreds" had been in training at Camp Nelson, just south of Louisville, and were untested in battle. There was racial dissension in the ranks as Burbridge's command moved south. Colonel James Brisbin, commander of the unit complained:

> "On the march, the colored soldiers, as well as their white officers, were made subject of much ridicule and many insulting remarks by the white troops, and in some instances petty outrages, such as pulling off the caps of colored soldiers, stealing their horses... insults, as well as the jeers and taunts that they would not fight." (Ibid, 115)

The Confederates had been alerted that Burbridge's army was on the way and quickly assembled a rag tag group of defenders from the various military and militia units from the area. Major General J. C. Breckenridge, a Kentuckian by birth, and Vice-President of the United States under James Buchanan, had at most seven regiments at his command in early October, 1864. Four of them were from Eastern Kentucky. Historian Henry Scalf wrote:

Gen. John C. Breckenridge, CSA

> "Now Kentuckians, brothers, neighbors and kinsmen were to meet in battle at Saltville as a fruition of their hate and bitterness. Each, Union and Confederate, went into battle, remembering the dark deeds charged to the other and their adherents back in the valleys and coves of the hills. Each remembered the guerrilla bands from which they or their kinsmen suffered. In their mind's eye they could see the burning cabins and towns." (DVA, 4)

By the night of September 29, Burbridge's army had reached the border separating Eastern Kentucky and Southwestern Virginia. There were few roads, making the passage extremely difficult for man and beast. "At least 8 men were killed when their horses stepped off the mountain road and they were thrown. It is not known how many were injured." (W–SWVA, 116) On the morning of September 30, the first contact was made. Colonel Edwin Trimble of Prestonsburg was in charge of the Confederate skirmishers and their intention was merely to slow Burbridge's progress, allowing more time for preparation in the defense of Saltville itself.

Burbridge was not aware that orders from General Sherman had been sent to call off the attack, but due to guerrilla activity to his rear, Burbridge received the order only after the battle. Some writers have speculated that Sherman made the decision because he was not in favor of recruiting colored soldiers for his army.

By the morning of October 2, the Confederates had been able to bring in two brigades and some artillery, approximately 1,700 men in all, to reinforce the 700 home guard, the fewer than 400 reserves, and the approximately 200 regulars already in place at Saltville. (Ibid, pp 117-118) The southern forces were outnumbered two to one, but they had the distinct advantage of defending the high ground above the Holston River, over which the Federals would have to cross in their attack. Tactically, Burbridge could not have chosen a worse approach. Before reaching the river, his troops would have to traverse fields of "briars, bushes, and wild corn, which were too low for cover, but high enough to slow the advance to a crawl." (Ibid, 119) This made them easy targets for the cannon emplacements on the bluffs. Additionally, the Holston River was too deep for favorable crossing except at one ford, and there were steep cliffs to negotiate for those who succeeded in making it across the river.

The battle for Saltville began at 11:00 on the morning of

October 2 with the Federals being repulsed repeatedly in their attempts to cross the river at the bluffs. General Burbridge, realizing the futility of that approach, sent several regiments to cross the Holston River further upstream to attack the Rebel defense from the dry land of the hills north of town. David Valentine's unit was in this group. They dismounted, leaving approximately 100 men behind to hold their horses. Also ordered into this flanking maneuver was the 5th Colored Mounted Infantry, which was sent to the front of the action and took heavy casualties. A Union surgeon's report listed the losses of this unit at 22 killed, 190 wounded, and 53 missing. (Ibid, 123)

The 39th KY was issued an average of 96 rounds of ammunition per man. The 5th U. S. Colored Mounted Infantry had been issued Enfield rifles which were very difficult if not impossible to load while on horseback, so they too, had dismounted. Additionally, they were mostly slave recruits with very little experience with firearms of any kind.

The northerners had superior firepower with their personal weapons. Many of the men had the new Spencer repeating rifles, or "carbines," while the southerners had mostly pistols and muzzle loader muskets which could fire at best 3 shots a minute. The Spencers held 7 shots and could fire 15 shots per minute with reloading. It was said the bullets could penetrate 13 inches into pine boards at 50 yards. At that juncture of the war, the South couldn't even use captured Spencers because they didn't have the facilities for manufacturing cartridges for them. (SWV-CV, 129)

Despite their advantage with weaponry, the battle was over by 5:00, when the Union forces ran out of ammunition and supplies just as they were about to claim victory. By that time, the orders from General Sherman to call off the attack had come through, so Burbridge departed the battlefield, leaving one of his field commanders to build campfires across the Holston River to give the impression that the Union forces were resting and would initiate a fresh attack the next morning. "As darkness covered the battlefield, the sound of musketry and cannon ceased. In the dark, the only sound coming from the field was the groans and moans of the wounded, mostly Northerners." (Ibid, 121)

Burbridge's expedition was deemed a complete failure, with total casualties of about 350. The only gain the officer could claim was the destruction of "some of the outer salt works.14

As the Union's beaten army retreated, the commanders had no choice but to leave behind their dead and wounded. The wounded, along with some attending medical officers and staff became Confederate prisoners. (OR, Ser. I, Vol. XXXIX. 553-554) It was an unwritten agreement that medical personnel were not usually treated as prisoners of war, and in a few days they were released and allowed to rejoin their units. One surgeon named William H. Gardner, who was attached to the Union 13th Kentucky Infantry, reported on October 26, that on October 3, the day after the battle, some men whom Gardner believed to be Confederate soldiers, came to the field hospital and shot five wounded men of the 5th U.S. Colored Cavalry, and later came to Emory and Henry College Hospital and shot several soldiers in their beds, including two more of the 5th U.S. Colored Cavalry, but also they were seeking to kill all of the wounded Union officers (Ibid, 554-555). Northern newspapers reported that 155 black soldiers had been massacred in the aftermath of the battle at Saltville. (W-SWVA, 122) These outrageous acts became the subject of many articles and books in later years.

---

14 Burbridge would return to Saltville as a subordinate officer in the successful second Saltville expedition two months later, and would be removed from command the following February. (LMOW, 274) His immense unpopularity in Kentucky due to his abuses and military failures prevented Burbridge from remaining in his native state. He relocated his family to New York and died there in 1894. (SM, 19)

Colonel James S. Brisbin, commander of the 5th U.S. Colored Cavalry, reported on Oct. 20 that of the 400 men of his unit who had been engaged in the battle (200 had been left behind the lines as sick and to hold horses) had suffered 114 men and 4 officers killed or wounded. He said of this fight, "I can only say that the men could not have behaved more bravely." (OR, Series I, Vol. XXXIX, 556-557)

A preliminary report on casualties at the battle of Saltville, issued on October 4, two days following the action, listed the 39th KY Mounted Infantry with 1 man killed and 10 wounded. The District surgeon who wrote the report conceded that the report was not totally reliable because many of the killed and wounded were left on the field when the Union forces withdrew on the evening of October 2. (Ibid, 553- 554)

Casualty figures for the 39th KY for the entire war period vary depending on the reporting source. The Compendium of the War of the Rebellion lists 3 officers and 24 enlisted men killed, and 194 enlisted men dead of disease. (OR-C, p 1721). John David Preston, quoting George Wolford, lists the 39th KY with 21 killed and 173 dead from "non-hostile causes such as smallpox, typhoid, and other diseases." (CW–BSV, 229)

CHAPTER X

CASUALTY

Sometime during that fateful day of October 2, 1864, Captain David Valentine Auxier suffered a bullet wound through his right lung. I say *through* his lung, because that was the report that came back from those who saw him during his brief stay in a makeshift field hospital.15 The projectile was likely a 58 caliber "Minnie" ball, which was known to wreak havoc on both soft and skeletal tissue. I have often wondered if David Valentine might have survived such a wound if it had occurred a hundred years later. In 1864, field surgeons were extremely limited in what could be done to save lives in cases of abdominal or thoracic trauma. History books are full of accounts of surgery tents being awash in blood from amputated limbs and repair of soft tissue wounds. The causes of infection were not understood at that time.

We have only one written account of the circumstances surrounding David's wounding and death two days later. Henry Scalf, the gifted historian and newspaper editor of *The Floyd County Times* of Prestonsburg, Kentucky, wrote a magnificent monograph on David Valentine as a part of an article entitled "Civil War Bitterness Flowered when East Kentuckians Fought," which was printed on April 13, 1961. (FCT) In view of the fact that we have no other detailed narrative of David Valentine's wounding and subsequent demise, and due to the fact that Scalf's account is so beautifully written, it is herein presented in its entirety:

> "They had not wanted to be there, but some strange allure of mixed patriotism and hate had brought them. Captain David Auxier had told his uncle, Major John B. Auxier, 'I feel like I will not return.' The Major had

---

15 During the disinterment of David Valentine's remains in 1991, no bullet was found in the grave.

replied that if he felt that way, perhaps it could be arranged that he did not go on the Virginia expedition.

Young David had shook his head, saying, 'I shall go.'

Soldiers remember their premonitions and it may be that David recalled his misgivings at Saltville, remembered it more vividly as he suffered from a chest wound on the field. Comrades carried him to a barn and left him with other wounded.

Darkness threw a mantle over the bloody field, and Burbridge, with several hundred casualties, began to disengage his troops. It was then that David's brother George had missed him, inquired to learn that he had been taken to the barn. George found the barn but David was gone. Friends had carried him to the nearby Powers farmhouse and put him to bed. Later they brought Lige Hensley, suffering from a leg wound, and placed him beside David.

That night Union medics, under the threat of imminent capture by the rampaging Confederates, visited the farmhouse at the prompting of Major Auxier. One look at David and they saw he would live but a short time. Hensley would live if his leg was amputated.

There in the near darkness, in the dim light of a kerosene lamp, the doctor braced Hensley with liberal amounts of whiskey and took off his leg. Hensley, enraged when he found his leg had been removed, cursed the doctor roundly. David, who had been praying, chided his companion, 'Don't say that, Lige.'

George Auxier found his brother at the farmhouse, (and) stood silently by as the crude battlefield amputation was performed on Hensley. He vowed to stay with David, but the wounded man demurred.

'No, George, you cannot.' David said, 'You will be taken prisoner.'

Major Auxier and George both realized David was

right. To stay would provide no help, as they saw death was not far away. They agreed to go, prolonging their farewells, listening for Confederate cavalry. Suddenly all the soldiers in the room began to weep.

'It was the first time I had seen soldiers weep over the death of a man,' Major Auxier said in the after years.

Hensley was still the bed companion of David Auxier when he died. He remembered how he suffered and prayed and the climactic clapping of David's hands, just before he expired. He had lived two days with that ugly hole in his chest.

Farm people came and took the body away for burial. Lige Hensley didn't know where.

News travels slowly in a mountain country devoid of communications, and war intensifies the difficulty of dissemination. Nathaniel Auxier, now approaching life's end, heard of his son's sacrifice only after several days delay.

David's grief-stricken wife vowed she was going to Virginia to see him buried with Christian rites. Protestations of the family that such a journey through a guerrilla-infested mountain country, and that by a woman with Union sympathies in Confederate territory, was hazardous, to say the least, failed to impress the young widow.

Nathaniel Auxier finally bowed to the wish of his bereaved daughter-in-law and sent the Rev. Robert Hurt, a friend of the family but a well-known Confederate sympathizer. Hurt, a Virginian by birth, knew scores of the officers and men on both sides. Nathaniel thought he would provide a safe escort for Elizabeth to the Saltville battlefield.

Winter was encompassing the mountains when Rev. Hurt and Elizabeth Auxier set out on horseback for

Powers family showed the widow an unmarked grave on the farm.

Hurt and Mrs. Auxier arranged to have the body exhumed and it was interred with appropriate rites in the McCready cemetery. They set a small stone, upon which had been inscribed the legend, 'D. Auxier,' and then they returned to Kentucky.

As the months wore away and peace returned, Mrs. Auxier again went to Virginia to visit her soldier-husband's grave. She was accompanied this time by the dead man's uncle, James W. M. Stewart.[16] In the decades that followed, residents in the vicinity of McCready cemetery recalled vividly the weeping widow of Kentucky.

Mrs. Auxier never went back. Childless, she went to her people in Greenup County and later remarried, moving to West Virginia where she died. No one in the Auxier family now knew where Capt. David Auxier was buried. Even the name of the cemetery slipped into the limbo of unremembered history." (DVA, pp 5 - 7) [17]

---

16 William Ely, author of *The Big Sandy Valley*, 1887, called him "James E. Stewart." Ely stated that Stewart, being a sympathizer with the Southern side, was imprisoned at Camp Chase for a year, was released by exchange, returned home, and became highly successful in law and business. He was district prosecutor for six years, followed by an equal term as Judge of the Criminal Court of his district. He married David Valentine's mother's sister, Cynthia Mayo. (BSV, 96)

17 This account is probably based on a letter written by Isaac Goble that was in the possession of Judge John Frew Stewart, Major and Adjutant of the 39th Kentucky at the time Stewart wrote his firsthand account of the 39th in 1906. A typescript of the Frew account, which mentions this letter as "attached," is among the Henry Scalf papers at the Allara Library at Pikeville College, Pikeville, Kentucky. The Goble letter has not been found.

On January 25, 1866, Elizabeth S. Childs filed a widow's claim for pension for the period October 4, 1864 to May 1, 1865. (USPO -1) She remarried to a man named Henry Childs on that latter date. 18 She included a copy of her marriage certificate to David Valentine Auxier and stated the particulars of his death at the battle of Saltville, Virginia. On March 9, 1866, the Adjutant General's Office sent her an acknowledgement of receipt of her claim. The only indication that Lizzie received any pension money for that claim is noted in her subsequent application in 1903, stating that "...my attorney at Cattlettsburg (KY) paid me money but I don't recollect how much." (USPO-2)

Elizabeth's second husband, Henry M. Childs, died on November 23, 1885, when the couple was living near Ripley, West Virginia. (USPO-4) Elizabeth married a third time, to Henry F. Chase, but according to her statement in a later pension affidavit dated Jan. 2, 1903, "My husband is very old and feeble and not able to provide for me and I am old also. I have no support or home and I am not able to work every day for my living. I own no home of my own. Now, what time I do live, could I receive my former husband's pension?" (USPO-2)

Accompanying her own affidavit in this pension application were several statements from neighbors and friends who had known Elizabeth during her later marriages, and one from Lt. Isaac Goble who served with David Valentine in the 39th Kentucky, was a fellow prisoner of the Confederates in Richmond, and who fought with him at Saltville. (USPO-6) There was also a document from the County Clerk of Jackson County, West Virginia, dated Aug. 14, 1905, certifying that Elizabeth and Henry Childs "... are neither assessed with real or personal property for the year 1904 – 1905." (USPO-5)

95

---

18 See appendix for photocopy of Elizabeth's pension application and affidavits on her behalf.

In 1906, family historian Agnes Auxier, received the following letter from the daughter of Elizabeth Auxier Childs:

"Allegheny City, Penn.
April 15, 1906

My Dear Friend,

Your letter came to hand several weeks ago, but my mother was dead and buried. She died the seventeenth of February, having been sick since last August. She was sick in bed when she was writing down there about her pension – she died of cancer of the liver.

She often talked about her first husband's people, how good and kind they were to her, and of her intended visit down there. I expected to go with her in the spring. I am the eldest child, there are five of us living; three of us are living in this city and one sister is living in West Virginia and a brother in Ohio.

My mother was married three times. My father, Henry Childs, died and left the children small; he did not leave any property as he drank. Later she married Henry Chase, who was a miller and he helped rear her little ones – I don't know anything of my mother's first husband, only as she told me. I have often heard her say that she could write a book of her past life – I send you my mother's [piocture and also that of her young husband, David Auxier.

Your friend,

Mrs. Helen Morton" (AH, 29)

Mabel Auxier Rice, niece of David Valentine, had possession of many of the papers and archives of Agnes Auxier the historian, including a typed manuscript of her 1908 history of the Auxier family I described in Chapter II. I asked for and received permission from Mabel's daughter, Mary Grace Garland, to search the material for anything pertaining to David Valentine, including the pictures that her daughter mentioned in the above letter. Unfortunately, the search did not reveal either of the photographs, and I still do not have a picture of David's wife.

CHAPTER XI

LOST AND FOUND

After Elizabeth's second trip to Saltville in early 1865, she never returned to her husband's burial site or to visit the Auxier family in the Big Sandy Valley of Kentucky. Childless, she went back to her birthplace in Greenup County, and as noted in the previous chapter, after two subsequent marriages, died at about age 60 of cancer of the liver in West Virginia.

Reverend Robert Hurt and James Stewart who had accompanied her on the two trips to Saltville after David's death, passed away, and the location of his grave was lost to the Auxier family.

Circumstances prevented David's brother George from retrieving the body from Virginia and returning it to his family cemetery in Kentucky. Their mother, Hester, had passed away on May 4, 1864, just six days after giving birth to Edward, the last of her children, and their father, Nathaniel, died on June 29, 1865. This left George, at age 23, and the oldest surviving son, as head of the family. There were ten younger brothers and sisters to care for, leaving no time for relocating the remains of his brother from a far-off cemetery. Such an undertaking would have been most difficult, considering the distance and lack of roads across the mountains at that time, not to mention the continued tension of Reconstruction and the depth of the scars left by the conflict. The year from May of 1864 to June of 1865 had been a devastating one for the Auxier family.

George wasted no time in acquiring a helpmate, marrying his double first cousin, Angeline Prater from Magoffin County. Angeline was the same cousin with whom David Valentine had corresponded before his death. George and "Ann" as she was called, were married on December 3, 1865, and began a large f family of their own the following year.

George's two younger brothers, Nathaniel and Edward, went to Nebraska in the 1880's to take advantage of the Homestead Act, providing free farm land for anyone willing to live on and cultivate an acreage in that undeveloped part of the country. David Valentine and his young bride had dreamed of owning "good land in the West," but Nat and Ed were the ones to see that dream come to fruition. Both of them became prosperous

Nathaniel
Auxier

farmers and ranchers. Ed organized and became president of a small bank at Verdon, Nebraska, and he was elected to the Nebraska state legislature.

Nathaniel and Edward no doubt had many conversations about David Valentine and perhaps wondered, as I did in later years, what the cemetery looked like and whether David's grave marker could still be found. Had the cemetery been properly cared for? All they really knew was that it was in a small community called "McCready,"and that it was near the town of Saltville. Their older brother George, who had served in David's company and had been forced to leave him mortally wounded on the battlefield, had died in 1895, and his wife Ann, who was their surrogate mother, lived until 1911.

Edward E.
Auxier

In 1926, sixty-two years after David Valentine fell in battle, Ed Auxier (who was called Uncle Ed by my family) returned for a visit to Kentucky. He and Garland Rice, (Garland married Ed's daughter, Mabel) who was also the grandson of the same Reverend Robert Hurt who had accompanied Elizabeth on her first trip to Saltville, boarded a train and went to Saltville to search for David's grave. They were unsuccessful. (DVA, 7)

In 1931, Garland and Mabel, and Joe and Anna Layne Davidson, were returning from Wilmington, North Carolina, when they decided to stop at Saltville. Mrs. Davidson was also a niece of David Valentine, although their forbears had opposed each other at the battle of Saltville. Lt. Greenville Davidson served in the 14th Regiment, Kentucky Volunteer Cavalry, CSA. (DVA, 7) 19 In 1961, Henry Scalf wrote the following about this search:

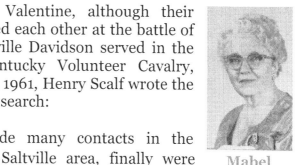

Mabel Auxier Rice

"They made many contacts in the Saltville area, finally were referred to an aged man, Curren Sanders, who,

Anna Layne Davidson

although he had lost an awareness of many things due to his years, was still wont to reminisce about the Battle of Saltville. He could not remember anything about the Auxier grave, he said, sadly shaking his head.

The party admitted defeat, were getting in their car when Mrs. Rice thought she might have the key that would unlock his memory. She asked him if he remembered a widow and a man coming from Kentucky decades ago, searching for a soldier's grave. He did not remember. Many people had searched for their sons and brothers.

The old man stood shaking his head as the visitors were starting to leave again. Then suddenly, the rush of memories came and he recalled the widow and her companion. They had found the grave on the Powers farm and removed the body to McCready cemetery. He remembered well, for the widow had wept long and deep.

---

19 John David Preston lists Davidson with the 5th Reg., KY Infantry,

CSA. (CW–BSV, 270)

Sanders took the party to the McCready cemetery, and they walked among the ancient graves. Many had imposing stones, many were unmarked. Sanders could not point out where Capt. Auxier was buried but he knew it was here.

It was Rice who found it. He removed the moss from what he believed was the head of a grave and examined a crude stone. Scratching away the lichens, he read, 'D. Auxier.'

This summer, 100 years less three after Capt. David Valentine Auxier died, his relatives in the Big Sandy Valley will once again journey to McCready cemetery to erect a large memorial. They will not remove the field stone, however, upon which Rev. Hurt inscribed a name while the sorrowing widow watched. It is too symbolic of the tragic years."(Ibid, 7-8)

There is no record that anything more was done about David Valentine's grave site until 1953 when Garland Rice wrote to my uncle, also named George Washington Auxier, an official with the U. S. Government in Washington, D. C., informing him that permission had been granted to erect a new marker on the grave. Apparently, George had ordered a bronze military marker, because in his note, Garland gave instructions about shipment of the marker to Saltville. The permit was signed by a Mrs. W. J. Totten, nearest of kin of the owner of the cemetery land, and Earnest I. McCready, grandson of the owner. It was witnessed by J. F. Clear, Jr., and William O. Clear. 20   It is not known when the marker was actually installed, but it was in place for the memorial service which took place at the McCready cemetery on August 5, 1961. Garland Rice and his wife, Mabel, were apparently the organizers because the printed program listed Garland as the person who made the introductions, and Mabel presented an

---

20 W. O. "Oscar" Clear would later be the key to locating the grave in 1990. See appendix for a copy of the permit.

"In Memoriam" during the ceremony. Also on the program was Anna Layne Davidson, who, along with her husband Joe, had accompanied the Rices when they found the grave thirty years earlier. (MEM) 21

The memorial service was attended by several members of the Auxier family and by officers and members of the Saltville-Preston Chapter of the United Daughters of the Confederacy. A welcome was extended by Mrs. V. T. Rector, Secretary of the U. D. C. chapter, speaking on behalf of Mrs. W. J. Totten, president:

"One hundred years ago the country in which we are now living was ripped and torn as if a kite in a hurricane. From each of the rips and tears flowed the brave blood of our courageous forefathers. This afternoon, we are here to pay tribute to one who gave the greatest sacrifice known to mankind, his life. May we, as Americans today, realize our own responsibilities to our children and the future generations of this country and do our part to keep this country free. On behalf of the Saltville-Preston Chapter of the United Daughters of the Confederacy and with deepest sympathy and respect, I extend to you a most sincere welcome to this memorial service." (Ibid)

Among those who attended the 1961 memorial service were, (L to R) Mabel Auxier Rice, Mrs. Walter Zurbrick, H. B. Rice, and Earnest McCready

103

---

21 See appendix for a copy of the cover of the 1961 memorial service.

The principal address was given by Henry Scalf, noted historian and editor of *The Floyd County Times* newspaper at Prestonsburg, Kentucky. 22 The following is an excerpt from that address:

> "If it were possible for the living to pierce the eternal veil separating us from the dead, I would address myself to Capt. David Valentine Auxier, in whose honor we dedicate this memorial stone.
>
> I would have him know that his kinsmen still remember, although a hundred years have gone, and while not a kinsman, I would say as a Kentuckian, that I remember, too, with great pride, for he personified Kentucky, its traditions of valor, sacrifice, honor and loyalty.
>
> The division of another century is gone and in its place there is a union of hearts. America is great with strength. That is the way Capt. Auxier wanted it. For that he made the supreme sacrifice.
>
> The words we utter now will not add to the record Capt. Auxier imprinted on the roll of history or left in the traditions of his people and we seek neither to add nor alter. The record is imperishable, transcending even this everlasting stone. Our words only ease our hearts.
>
> Our remembrance is the *raison d'etre* of this stone but when our words are uttered, the prayers said and the memorial wreath left to the summer sun, the stone itself will forever remain the symbol of a charge. Be faithful and guard. Offer yourselves as watchful sentinels. America is great for its defenders sacrificed, even life itself.
>
> Capt. David Valentine Auxier, your Kentucky kinsmen, and the Virginians upon whose soil you died, salute you." (Ibid)

---

22 This book was dedicated to the memory of Henry Scalf.

Mabel Rice read the "In Memoriam." Anna Layne Davidson placed a wreath on the grave, and the service was concluded with a prayer by Mrs. Ruth Davidson Sowards, another niece of David Valentine. (Ibid) 23

Included in the printed program was a note of appreciation for Miss Minnie Frye and Earnest McCready:

> "It was Miss Minnie Frye who lead us to the cemetery where the grave of Capt. Auxier was located...While at the grave, some thirty years ago, Miss Minnie told us, 'Mother told us to always remember the soldier's grave on Decoration Day, for he was a good man.' On succeeding visits to the cemetery, Miss Minnie would join us as often as she could and we would always find the grave properly cared for, as though it were of her own. Her gracious hospitality will be gratefully remembered.
>
> We are indeed indebted to Earnest [McCready] for his fine cooperation in helping make this occasion possible. Preparation of the cemetery, placing of the marker, taking us to the battlefield, entrenchments, salt kettles, and other kindnesses too numerous to mention, we very deeply appreciate." (Ibid)

Also attending the 1961 memorial service were three of my aunts, Mrs. Anna A. Dorton, Miss Madge Auxier, and Mrs. Gertrude Holbrook. Another notable was Douglas Auxier Galbraith, owner and editor of *The Paintsville Herald*.

With the passing of the Auxier contingent who witnessed the 1961 ceremony at the grave site at Saltville, the location once again lapsed into the "lost" category. If there were children present, they were not mentioned in the programs and newspaper accounts, and even if there were small children present, they would likely have been too young to remember landmarks. Another thirty years passed.

---

23 See appendix for a copy of Mrs. Sowards' prayer.

CHAPTER XII

FOUND AGAIN

On November 15, 1990, almost thirty years after the dedication of the bronze military marker on David Valentine's grave, my wife, Eileen, and I were driving from our home in Memphis to Virginia Beach, Virginia, for a conference. We got an early start from the Knoxville area on the second leg of the trip, and since it was going to be a leisurely drive, I suggested we stop at Saltville to see if we could find the McCready Cemetery. According to the map, Saltville was only a few miles off the interstate. I had never been to Saltville and was curious about the condition of the cemetery and the general features of the valleys and hills where the battle took place. Perhaps we would get lucky in locating David Valentine's grave.

We stopped to ask directions, and learned that the community of McCready was on Highway 91, about two miles east of town. The settlement was very ordinary looking, but there was a Chevron station owned and operated by a man named Oscar Clear. Mr. Clear's son, a middle-age man, had lived in that community all his life but had never heard of the McCready Family Cemetery. He summoned his father, who declared that "Yes, he knew where it was located." I later found Mr. Clear's name as a witness on the permit to place David Valentine's bronze military grave marker several decades earlier.**24**

I will be eternally grateful for Mr. Oscar Clear. Without this fortuitous meeting, I would probably not be writing this book. The constraint of time would not have allowed much more research to locate the cemetery, and in retrospect, there was a good chance I would never have returned to renew the effort. Mr. Clear told us the graveyard had long since been abandoned, but it was situated on the side of a steep hill just up the road from the store. He indicated that it was on private

------

24 See appendix for a copy of the permits to place the marker.

property behind some houses that had were built into the slope, and that we should knock on the door of a certain house to get permission to go through their yard and up the hill to the site. We thanked him for the information and made our way to the row of houses he had indicated. We were fortunate to find someone home at the designated house, and our requested permission was granted.

An old gravestone in the McCready cemetery

Gravestone adjacent to DVA's marker

There was no road up the bluff, and we had to maneuver through a tangle of bushes and briars. Reaching the area that looked like it might have been a graveyard.

Eileen and I tramped around through the undergrowth and located a few ancient stones, mostly covered by vines, moss, and lichens. The cemetery was so overgrown that a rabbit hunter could have passed through it without realizing it was once a neat and well cared-for family burying place. We later learned that there had been only two burials there in the past century.

We located about two dozen gravestones before finding the handsome bronze marker on David Valentine's grave. I was pleased that it was in good condition, and that its elevation from the ground had prevented it from being covered with the leaves of late fall. What a thrill to finally see what I had only imagined for so many years!

I took some pictures of the marker and some of the

108

DVA bronze military marker

adjacent stones, and we were still milling about the vicinity of our significant discovery when my foot struck a stone covered in the leaves a few feet below David Valentine's grave. I kicked off the leaves, and bending down for a

closer look, read a crudely chiseled epitath, "*D. AUXIER.*" Needless to say, I was exhilarated to find that long-lost gravestone, carved by some 19th century hand, long forgotten, and with *my* name on it! (A reminder to my readers - I had been named for David Valentine Auxier). The hair rose on the back of my neck as I realized the implications of the moment.

Eileen with DVA gravestones

Since that occasion in that small family cemetery at Saltville, I cannot tell the story without becoming emotional. This was the beginning of an obligation I needed to fulfill in order to exorcise the ghosts that had haunted my psyche after learning that my great grandfather, George Washington Auxier, had been forced to leave his mortally wounded brother on the battlefield on October 2, 1864.

Eileen helped me regain my composure, and we prepared to return to our car at the foot of the hill. The field stone marker was relatively small, measuring roughly 12" by 18" by 3", and being fearful the precious stone would once again be lost, I made a decision to take it with me back to Memphis.

I did not reveal to Eileen until we were back on the road that I had an important plan for David Valentine's marker. I told her, "I'm going to dig up my great, great uncle and move his remains back to Kentucky." She said, "You're going to do WHAT?" Eileen is a very reasonable Southern girl and after 35 years of marriage, she had become accustomed to many of my unusual pursuits and actions. That day, she let me know in no uncertain terms that this idea was in her opinion, *preposterous.* I countered with the posit that David Valentine was one of my family's most famous heroes and should not have to languish in an obscure abandoned cemetery in another state for the remainder of eternity. I reminded her that I had been named after David, and felt a certain responsibility in that regard. The discussion ended without a meeting of the minds, and after the conference at Virginia Beach, we returned to Memphis with a moldering gravestone in the trunk of the car and a burning idea in the mind of the author of this book.

Soon after, I began a journal, sensing that a written record of the events along the way would be helpful in my campaign to win the hearts and minds of my relatives in carrying out my plan. The journal continued until August 31, 1991, and eventually filled a yellow legal pad with dates and notes. It was a good decision.

I began a letter-writing campaign to apprise my history-minded relatives of my intentions. At first, the response was less than positive. My brother Bob, and my Aunt Madge, sided with Eileen, thinking that too much time had elapsed since David Valentine's death, and that I should let him rest in peace in Virginia. On December 12, I wrote a follow-up letter, stating that the deplorable condition of the cemetery could not be properly appreciated without going there in person. I reiterated my zeal for the project, listing six strong reasons for proceeding. They were: (1) I was the only living relative (other than Aunt Madge who had attended the 1961 dedication ceremony, and was then 92 years old), who knew the location of David's grave; (2) the cemetery was so obscure that some of the younger local residents didn't even know about it; (3) the cemetery had long since been abandoned by the McCready family; (4) Capt. Auxier was, to my knowledge, our only kinsman who had lost his life in the Civil War, and if his position in history was to have any meaning, his remains and markers would have to be relocated; (5) I believed that the government would pay for the expense of relocation of David Valentine's remains; and, (6) there were several good reasons why his family had not already made an effort to bring him back to Kentucky. My final exhortation in the letter was to "please think on these things and let me know if you still believe his (David Valentine's) present situation is fit and proper for one of our own who gave his life in the service of his country."

In the next few weeks, resistance to my proposal began to soften. One aunt had been under the impression that David was buried in a national cemetery at Saltville. As the network of correspondence expanded, I began to receive some support, and by January, 1991, there was a groundswell of enthusiasm not only for the relocation, but also for my suggestion that we have a second memorial for David Valentine at his re-burial location in Kentucky.

On January 10, I called the Smyth County, Virginia, Health Department to inquire about the requirements for exhuming David's remains and transferring them back to Kentucky. They informed me that the disinterment would have to be done by a licensed funeral home, and that a permit would be required to transport the remains across the state line from Virginia.

I then called Oscar Clear at the Chevron station to ask his advice for hiring a local funeral home. Without hesitation, he recommended the Henderson Funeral Home, a second-generation business presently owned by David Henderson. Mr. Henderson was an excellent choice, in that he was not only a consummate professional funeral director, but was also a Civil War buff who was more than willing to share his knowledge of the battle of Saltville. He readily agreed to arrange for the necessary permits. We tentatively set a date for the disinterment for February 18, weather permitting.

After several phone calls to Johnson County, Kentucky, I made contact with the manager of the Johnson County

Memorial Cemetery at Staffordsville, where David Valentine's brother, George and other relatives were buried.25 I reserved a plot about twenty feet from that of George. The cost would be $325.00 for the plot, plus $50 to $80 to re-inter the remains, and $20 to re-set the bronze military marker. I also asked the manager to cast a cement marker for the small fieldstone marker that I had retrieved from the McCready cemetery.

The final step in the relocation process would be to engage the services of a local funeral home in Johnson County. My cousin, the late Paul Cecil Auxier, who was on the board of directors of Johnson County Memorial Cemetery, recommended the Paintsville Funeral Home. They agreed to handle the arrangements for tents and chairs for the memorial service at a date to be determined later.

---

25 This family cemetery had been relocated when the Paintsville Lake dam was built in 1983, and all the properties above the dam were claimed by the Corps of Engineers.

CHAPTER XIII

RELOCATION

I called David Henderson on February 15 to check on the permits for opening the grave and moving David's remains to Kentucky. 26 He said he had them, and gave me an estimate of what it would cost for his own services. Some years earlier I had taken up the hobby of metal-detecting, so I asked him about utilizing a metal detector during the dig. David, being a detector hobbyist himself, endorsed the plan and offered to bring in a local man named Harry Haynes who was highly skilled with that electronic instrument. Harry, it turned out, was a wizard at the art and craft of metal detecting, and had assembled an impressive collection of bullets, bayonets, cannon balls, and other artifacts from the Saltville battlefield. I was happy to have a more experienced detectorist on the scene. Henderson ended the call by adding that the local historical society might want an interview for the Saltville newspaper. I agreed.

As the time drew near for the expedition to Southwestern Virginia, I nervously watched the weather forecast for that region. On the day before my scheduled departure from Memphis, it did not look at all favorable, with cold rain or snow in the forecast. Henderson had assured me that if the ground was frozen, we could get the equipment up the hill to the cemetery. The arrangements had all been made and since the schedules for everyone concerned was tight, I decided the mission was a "*GO.*"

Leaving Memphis at 1:30 p.m. on the 16th, I drove to Lafollette, Tennessee, a few miles north of Knoxville, where my sister Wanda's home would serve as a staging area for the final leg of the trip. My son Randy, then a doctoral candidate in philosophy at Emory University in Atlanta, (he would defend his dissertation a year later), had asked to join me in

---

26 See appendix for copy of the permits to move DVA's remains.

the mission. As an ardent student of Civil War history, and having taken a great interest in the David Valentine story, Randy had spent considerable time in libraries, searching the massive 126 volume "*Official Record of the War of the Rebellion*" series for any references to David Valentine Auxier, his regimental unit, and the battle of Saltville. 27 His efforts were fruitful and he brought with him several packets of printouts for future reference.

We left our rendezvous stopover at Lafollette at 8:30 a.m. on the 17th in a freezing rain. The roads were clear, however, and we arrived at Saltville at 1:30 that afternoon This is the same James Abram Garfield that later became the 20th president of the United States.

The roads were still bad by the standards of the late 20th century, but I am sure that David Valentine's young wife Elizabeth would have found them easy passage. When we arrived, David Henderson had an appointment, so we ate lunch and went back to the funeral home to wait. After cordial greetings and casual conversation about the weather prospects for the next day, David took Randy and me on a tour of Saltville, giving us a brief history of the town as we drove. He related that the salt works had closed after the war. In the late 1880's, the Olin Mathison Company came in and built a factory for manufacturing caustic soda. During World War I, the company made ingredients for chemical warfare, and eventually closed its doors in 1971. The primary industry of Saltville at the time we were there was a factory which made wheels for large road grading equipment.   Turning our attention to points of interest about the battle, David showed us old gun emplacements, fortifications, and entrenchments

114

---

27 These days such research is easy, since the entire record is on-line and searchable at Cornell University, but that was not the case in 1991

which were in place in 1864. Prominently displayed at the entrance of the city cemetery was a Confederate cannon, which David said was used in the battle. The cemetery itself is located on a high bluff overlooking the North Fork of the Holston River. The bluff was the center of the ill-fated assault across the river by elements of General Burbridge's Union forces. Confederate Colonel Edwin Trimble of Prestonsburg, Kentucky, was killed on this spot early in the battle.

David Henderson shows Randy a Confederate cannon used in the Battle of Saltville

The final stop onDavid Henderson's tour was to McCready, to give us another look at the cemetery and to enable us to finalize our plans for approaching the gravesite. It woulod not be easy, since snow was already falling that afternoon.

Returning to Saltville, Randy and I ate supper at a local restaurant and accepted Henderson's invitation to play some pool in a room he owned near the funeral home. David showed us his 1966 Corvette, his bass boat, his collection of antiques including a rebuilt 19th century snow sleigh, and some old cash registers and farm tools.

The next morning, February 18, we convoyed to the McCready Cemetery, with David Henderson pulling his "Ditch Witch" backhoe on a low-boy trailer. It was raining, but the ground was still frozen enough to maneuver the backhoe into position. Harry Haynes was already on site, and Jerry Roberts, an employee of the funeral home, assisted with the equipment. A local

Henderson's backhoe

historian, Tom Totten, arrived, took some pictures, and asked me some questions, presumably for the local newspaper or historical society.

Henderson, knowing the traditional methods of the local

populace in burying their dead, quickly determined on which side of David Valentine's bronze marker to dig. After fine-tuning the location of the backhoe to its best advantage, the marker was lifted aside and the digging began.

Jerry Roberts, Harry Haynes, and David Henderson

Four feet of soft dirt was removed before Harry Haynes indicated that he was beginning to get some faint signals from his metal detector. The pace slowed, and soon after, all the dirt removal was done by shovel, checking each scoopful as it was retrieved from the grave. This process continued for some time with nothing of significance found before it was time to break for lunch. David Henderson had thoughtfully brought along some delicious sandwiches for the crew.

After lunch, several local residents appeared at the site, including Elizabeth Frye, sister of George Frye who, along with Earnest McCready and his two sons, had cleaned off the area around David Valentine's grave for the 1961 dedication ceremony. Mrs. Frye remembered the Rice family from Paintsville, Kentucky, coming to Saltville in a black Cadillac many years earlier to visit the gravesite.

A cold rain settled upon the cemetery, making the work difficult and miserable. David and his workers stretched a large tarpaulin over the grave and backhoe. We continued working in semi-comfortable conditions. At around a depth of five feet, Harry started finding "square" nails, which were the kind used during the Civil War and beyond. These were angular in design as opposed to the round nails which came to

Vault in floor of grave

116

popularity later. A few more shovels of dirt, and the men at the bottom of the grave hit bedrock. But this wasn't ordinary bedrock. As we began to clear the dirt that was above the rock, an unexpected sight was revealed. To everyone's astonishment, a vault had been hand-
chiseled into the stone to conform to the physical dimensions of the person being buried. The vault was wide at the shoulder and narrow at the feet, and approximated David Valentine's height of five feet, seven inches, (according to his enlistment papers). From the standpoint of disinterment, this was a great stroke of luck. It was a perfect template for determining where to locate the teeth, leg bones, and buttons. *And locate, we did*!

Our anticipation grew with each shovel full of dirt that came out of the grave. Harry frequently admonished us to "Be careful, this one has a button in it," or "This one should have some teeth in it." The bones we found were essentially deteriorated beyond recognition except for some fragments of long bones from the legs and a piece of a knee joint. Square nails were in abundance, but the wood of the burial box had long since rotted away. Thirteen of David Valentine's teeth were recovered. David Henderson advised us that the rich, dark earth in the bottom of the vault *was* David Valentine, and that we should save this soil for his re-interment.

To our great delight, seven Union Infantry officer's buttons and a section of a braided captain's shoulder insignia gave us the proof we needed that we had indeed located the remains of my long lost great, great uncle, David Valentine Auxier. Amazingly, the heavy cloth backing of some of the buttons survived those twelve and a half decades in the cold, damp ground, making the trove even more precious.

Nails from DVA's coffin

U.S. Infantry officer's buttons from DVA's tunic

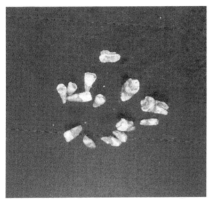

DVA's teeth from gravesite at Saltville

Close-up of DVA's coat button

I had hoped to find David Valentine's wedding ring, but there was always a question about whether he ever had one, and if so, whether his wife, Elizabeth, had removed it during the first exhumation after the battle. Additionally, there was a remote possibility that the fatal bullet might still be in the grave. The reports by David's brother George and his uncle, John B. Auxier, were that the bullet had penetrated all the way through his chest. The rifles used by both sides of the war were extremely powerful and the 58 caliber "Minnie" balls would not have been stopped by mere flesh and bone. Aside from these minor disappointments, I could not have been happier with the results of the day's work.

After carefully bagging the Captain's teeth and bones, and loading some of the rich, dark earth, into a heavy black plastic bag, I took pictures of the vault at the bottom of the grave and of the crew and the site in general. We filled in the grave, pulled out the equipment, and headed back to town. Back on the road, I stopped at the Chevron station to tell Oscar Clear we had achieved our mission and to thank him for helping me find the cemetery and for recommending the Henderson Funeral Home. Harry Haynes suggested we also stop to see Mrs. Grace McCready, wife of Earnest, who had died three years earlier. She received us graciously and I thanked her for the many kindnesses the McCready and Frye families had extended to the Auxiers over the years.

Back at the funeral home, we met Allen F. Frye who was an elderly employee of Henderson's. He remembered Mabel Rice and Annie Layne Davidson and their husbands when they came and found David Valentine's grave in 1931. Mr. Frye said he was about 11 or 12 years old at that time. He also related that the two women had later returned to Saltville and stayed with his great aunt, Minnie Frye during their visit.

David Henderson told us that, as far as he knew, other than David Valentine and the soldiers buried in the city cemetery in Saltville, there was only one other grave of a Civil War soldier in Smyth County. That one was for a Confederate who had died of smallpox on the return trip to Kentucky after the battle. Many local people knew about David Valentine and more or less adopted him as "our Yankee soldier." Although their allegiance to the Southern cause never wavered, I sensed that that they were reluctant to lose him.

Randy and I ate supper, I settled up with David Henderson, paying him a fair sized bonus for faithfully completing the project under extenuating weather circumstances, and we departed for Kentucky with David Valentine's remains and his ponderous bronze military marker safely in the trunk of the car. 28 Reaching the Kentucky line late that night, we had planned to stay at the Breaks of the Sandy Interstate State Park at the crest of the mountain. To our dismay, it was closed for the winter. We kept driving until we found an open motel on the Kentucky side, and spent the rest of the night there. I took some pictures of David Valentine's teeth while Randy read from a philosophy book, and we turned in, reveling in the accomplishments of the day.

As we resumed our journey the next morning, the fog was too thick to be able to see the spectacular view of the Breaks of the Sandy that I had heard so much about as a child growing up in Eastern Kentucky. My family had made an attempt to reach the summit on one Sunday excursion, but a summer rain had made the dirt road impassable. I have yet to see the Breaks of the Sandy.

The fog had dissipated as we passed through Pikeville and Prestonsburg on the way to our destination at Paintsville in Johnson County. I had previously arranged to meet my brother Bob, along with cousins Mary Grace Garland and John David Preston, so they were waiting for us. Mary Grace was the daughter of Mabel and Garland Rice who found David Valentine's grave in 1931, and John David is an attorney - he was mayor of Paintsville at the time. John was another great

---

28 See appendix for copy of the receipt for David Henderson's services.

nephew of David Valentine Auxier, having descended from David's uncle, Major John B. Auxier. John David's book on the Civil War in the Big Sandy Valley (which grew from his Harvard undergraduate thesis in history) is among the major historical sources for this book. I will say more about Mary Grace and John David later.

I transferred the bag with David Valentine's remains to Eugene Sturgill, the manager of the Johnson County Memorial Cemetery. He said he would construct a small sturdy wooden box for the remains, and we made arrangements to witness the reburial at the cemetery the next day. I

DVA's new footstone with original marker

had brought along the small fieldstone with "D. Auxier" inscribed on it, and I asked Sturgill if he could have a concrete casement molded around the stone to be used as the marker at the foot of David's grave. He readily agreed.

At dinner that evening, the group discussed a possible memorial service for David Valentine at his new and *presumably final* resting place. One large branch of the local Auxier family had been having a reunion on Memorial weekend every year, so it seemed to be the logical time for the proposed memorial. Preston agreed to send out announcements, arrange for a banquet, and coordinate the event. He also agreed to try to arrange for an honor guard and get media coverage for the ceremony. I later talked him into giving the major address at the memorial service. John David Preston, I learned, was a man who would deliver what he promised.

My brother Bob, an accomplished wood worker, agreed to frame the seven buttons we had retrieved from the grave. I wanted them mounted individually for presentation to special recipients to be named later. He said he would use some cherry wood he had saved from our old farm on Paint Creek just a mile above the Paintsville Lake Dam. Mary Grace agreed to place the wreath on David's grave at the ceremony, just as her mother, Mabel, had done at the 1961 ceremony.

Re-interment of DVA's remains

After observing the reburial of the remains at the cemetery the next day, Randy and I drove back to Lafollette, Tennessee, where his wife, Gaye, was waiting to take him back to Atlanta. The next morning, I drove back to Memphis, my mind filled with thoughts of what had transpired and what we had planned for Memorial weekend. There was a sort of euphoria – we had done a very unusual thing, after all -- but there was also a bit of apprehension about how the relocation of our family hero would be received.

CHAPTER XIV

COUNTDOWN

The next three months were spent promoting the memorial service, encouraging cousins from far and near to attend, and asking them to bring along any memorabilia and artifacts relating to David Valentine. I received a promise for a large original portrait of David Valentine from a cousin in Nebraska, along with his certificate of appointment as a third lieutenant in the 39ᵗʰ Kentucky Voluntary Infantry. There were also offers to bring the original letters that David Valentine had written to his father and to his cousin Angeline Prater.

On March 5ᵗʰ, I called the Regional Office of the Veterans Administration to ask if they could furnish an honor guard for the memorial service. They informed me that honor guards did not fall under the VA's responsibilities, suggesting that I call the Memphis Chapter of the Veterans of Foreign Wars. They in turn, referred me to the National Cemetery at Memphis. This got another referral to the Army base at Ft. Campbell, Kentucky, which relayed me to Ft. Knox, also in Kentucky. *Bingo!* They said they could furnish a rifle squad, color guard, and bugler. I would have to supply my own flag. I was given instructions for making a written request.

Four days later, I received a letter from John David Preston stating that he had sent out 80 announcement letters including information about local motels. He was concerned that the only banquet hall available for the gathering on the evening before the service would seat only 80 people. He also asked me for more information about David Valentine for his speech at the memorial.

Soon after, I called the National Cemetery at Memphis to inquire about securing a flag. They informed me that they could furnish a casket size 50 state flag, but on learning the purpose of the memorial, suggested that I purchase a Civil

War era banner from a flag manufacturer. Good idea! After some research, I settled on a 3 foot by 5 foot nylon 35 star flag with embroidered stars and sewn stripes. The cost was $48.00, and the manufacturer was, appropriately, "The Betsy Ross Flag Company." The 35 star flag was in use by the nation in 1864 when David Valentine was serving his country. 29

The 35 star Civil War flag

By the end of March, I had heard from several relatives who were enthusiastic about the proposed honor guard ceremony and were planning to make the trip to Kentucky. Some were coming from as far away as California and Oregon, with a sizeable contingent from Missouri. It was about this time that I began to think about family genealogy, and drew up some crude charts on large white poster boards, using what little information I could glean from Agnes Auxier's 1908 history of the Auxier family. I acquired some blank genealogy sheets from a friend and mailed them out to some of the cousins on John David Preston's address list. I had no idea where that idea might lead. Little did I know at the time, that I had created a monster that would consume most of my time and energy for the next nine years. I published the first edition of *"The Auxier Family" in 1995,* and the second edition containing 39,058 names in 2000.

On April 10th, I called Ft. Knox to confirm the honor guard

---

29 The Union Civil War flag (33 Star Flag) flew over Fort Sumpter. At the outbreak of the Civil War (1861), the U.S. Flag had a field of 33 stars representing 33 states. President Lincoln refused to remove the stars representing those states which seceded from the Union. From the first 3 months until 1863, the flag had 34 stars. In 1863, West Virginia separated from Virginia to join the Union. Consequently the Union flag had 35 stars until the close of the Civil War.

and was disappointed to learn that they could not commit to sending a unit that far ahead of the event. The lady I spoke with apprised me of the fact that since my request was for Memorial weekend, there might be applications for ceremonies for soldiers who had died very recently and they would have a higher priority than for a casualty that occurred 126 years earlier. It was difficult for me to concur with that position, but there was nothing I could do except wait, hoping for the best. I wrote to John David to inform him that we might have a problem. He said he would try to round up some local Civil War re-enactors to fire their rifles and fold the flag. This could be a backup plan if Ft. Knox didn't come through.

A week later, I received a letter from the Veterans Administration, rejecting my claim for reimbursement of my expenses for relocating David Valentine's remains from Virginia to Kentucky. Mysteriously, they wrote that I had failed to respond to their request for additional information *within one year of their request.* I wrote them back, reminding them that the request was not even submitted until February 22, 1991. This was the first of several miscommunications with various governmental agencies.

By the end of April, I was beginning to get really nervous about the honor guard situation. John David had struck out in securing re-enactors for the assignment. I called Ft. Knox again and was told they couldn't give me a definite answer until May 23.

Yet, things began to come together, so on May 3, I wrote to David Henderson and Harry Haynes at Saltville, inviting them to be my guests at the memorial service on May 26.

Two weeks later, my brother Bob called. He had finished the seven frames for the buttons and other relics from the Saltville battle.

Finally, on May 21st, my contacts at Ft. Knox called and committed to sending an honor guard unit, but said they were having trouble locating a bugler to blow "Taps." I thought, "How can we have an honor guard ceremony without "Taps?"

I asked my son Randy, who had not played trumpet since early high school, to give it a try, but in practice, he fractured enough notes that I decided that would not do for such a solemn occasion.

On May 24th, Eileen and I left Memphis for a stopover at my sister Wanda's home at Lafollette, Tennessee. Randy and Gaye were already there from Atlanta, and my sister Opal from California arrived soon after. My other siblings and their families would proceed directly to Paintsville on their own.

We all left LaFollette the next day in convoy, arriving at Paintsville mid-afternoon. John David had been able to reserve a larger hall that would seat 138 for the banquet that evening. I set up my genealogy charts, Bob's newly created button frames, and a display of various pictures and documents that had been previously promised.

126 people attended the banquet

By the facility's management count, 126 people attended the banquet. John David's seven-month-old daughter, Ellen Marie, was the youngest in attendance, and my mother, Bess, at 95, was the oldest.

For the program, I showed slides and talked about the relocation of David's Valentine's remains, followed by a session in which we passed the microphone around the room, asking each group to identify themselves and tell where they were from. My nephew, Maurice Dean Taylor of Missouri, closed the program with a stirring recitation of "The Ragged Old Flag," with accompanying patriotic music.

May 26th was the big day! After breakfast, George A. Auxier, great grandson of Major John B. Auxier of the 39th Kentucky Volunteer Infantry Regiment, led several of our group on a tour of the Blockhouse Bottom, where our ancestor, Samuel Auxier I had lived. It is a storied place, one of the earliest permanent English settlements in Kentucky, and our progenitor had even hosted Daniel Boone during the winter of 1796 −97.

On the way, I stopped to visit with Geneva Crider, a cousin who had possession of Agnes Auxier's papers and the books she had used in preparing the 1908 history of the Auxier family. Geneva promised to send me copies of anything she found related to David Valentine.

After a quick lunch, it was time to head to the Johnson County Memorial Cemetery for the honor guard ceremony.

CHAPTER XV

DAVID VALENTINE'S DAY

The two tents set up near the gravesite were already filled to near capacity when my family and I arrived at the Johnson County Memorial Cemetery which occupies a knoll below the dam at Paintsville Lake. It was just minutes before the two o'clock starting time for the service. I made a quick estimate that over 200 people had assembled for this graveside memorial service for my great, great, uncle, Captain David Valentine Auxier. I was concerned about having enough shelter and chairs, based on the

Civil War flag used at the 1991 honor guard service

number of Auxier kin who had attended the family reunion banquet in Paintsville the night before. 30

My present anxiety was an extension of the long distance fretting which had been building for several months. After all, this gathering of the clan and memorial service for Uncle David, was my idea, and I was sure that everyone present would hold me personally responsible for their comfort and protection from the elements. I had lived in these Eastern Kentucky mountains for a number of years and was painfully familiar with the beastly heat and humidity that could prevail on any given May 26th in the area, or the sudden rain shower that could send us scurrying for cover right in the middle of the service.

But why should *I* be concerned? Everything else had gone smoothly this weekend, and today, there was not a cloud in

129

---

30 By coincidence, there were 126 people at the banquet – one for every year since David Valentine was killed in battle.

the sky. Oh, it was hot, but the people who established this relocated cemetery had the good sense to place it on the top of a beautiful knoll where any breeze, from any direction, would be beneficial. We were blessed with some air movement today, and after setting up the 35 star "Civil War" American flag on a borrowed Boy Scout standard and pedestal, I noticed that the small gusts gave "Old Glory" just the right amount of ripple to create a good effect.

Everything seemed to be in order. I got my first look at the printed program for the service, and it had been well-prepared. 31I noted that reporters and cameramen from two television stations were on hand to cover the event. Cousin Howard Dorton, a retired surgeon from Lexington, joined several others in videotaping the proceedings. Others were taking snapshots of the gravestones and of each other, while some merely huddled in small groups to shake the hands and hug the necks of relatives they had not seen for many years. My 93 year old Aunt Madge, and my 95 year old mother, Bess, took seats of honor on the front row under one of the tents, and the relatives and friends found their niches wherever they could find some shade. I went over last minute details with the commander of the Honor Guard detachment from the Ft. Knox Army Base, and it was time to begin.

Author's mother Bess and Aunt Madge Auxier

The Invocation

I wanted my brother Bob to give the invocation for several reasons. He is, first

---

31 See appendix for copy of the cover of the 1991 DVA service.

of all, a deeply religious man who believes and lives the precepts of the Bible. Secondly, he is an Auxier who understands the importance of family history and the recognition of the contribution of its heroes. Third, he is a veteran whose faithful service on the U.S.S. Indiana in the Pacific Theater of the Second World War gives him a profound appreciation of our kinsmens' sacrifice than can be grasped by those who have not served in battle. Lastly, I felt that

Brother Bob
Auxier

Bob needed and wanted to have a part in this ceremony as a sort of penance for voicing some misgivings about the wisdom of moving the remains and markers of our great, great, uncle. Bob had quickly changed his mind after viewing pictures of the abandoned cemetery in Southwest Virginia where David Valentine had languished in near total obscurity for over twelve decades. Bob had in fact, become one of my biggest supporters of the project, for which I will always be grateful.

Sentimentality seems to be a common trait in my family, and both Bob and I had doubts about our ability to maintain composure as we stood before this assembly on this solemn occasion. I recalled the humility that my Uncle George Auxier must have felt when he was rendered speechless by a flood of memories during a visit to the one-room school that he had attended some 50 years earlier. 32

Bob and I had agreed in our planning sessions that it would be prudent to get our parts over early, that is, *before* the Honor Guard segment with the firing of the rifles, the playing of "Taps," and the folding and presentation of the flag. Even

131

---

32 My uncle George Auxier held a PhD in history and an important government job in the Executive Office Building next door to the White House in Washington, D.C.

with that plan, Bob struggled with the first few sentences of his invocation which he had obviously spent a great deal of time composing. His words soon began to flow freely and the prayer was beautiful.

"We are thankful, Heavenly Father, that you are allowing us the privilege of witnessing this Memorial Service which honors the memory of one of our ancestors who fell on one of the many battlefields of the American Civil War.

We are hereby reminded of the awful sacrifice by Captain David Valentine Auxier, who among so many others, gave of themselves so unselfishly in order to preserve this great Union of States and to provide freedom to those who for so long had been held under the terrible bondage of slavery.

Our Holy Scriptures record the words of our Lord and Savior, Jesus Christ, who said, 'Greater love has no man than this, that a man lay down his life for his friends.' We do, therefore, humbly acknowledge their sacrifice in giving their last full measure of devotion to God and Country.

Ours is the heritage of their offering on our behalf. We hereby do steadfastly resolve by Your grace and mercy to hold fast to the principles for which they died.

We beseech Your continued blessing upon this great nation. Cleanse us from our many flaws, failures, and shortcomings. Keep us strong in faith and trust, depending upon You to bring us safely through troubled times, as You have so graciously done in the past. Father, direct our paths as individuals and as a nation, so that our efforts will be blessed by You and that we may enjoy the fruits of Your benefits.

Cause us Lord, not only to be ever mindful of what they did in securing the blessings of liberty for ourselves and our posterity, but teach us to recognize and acknowledge that it was You who brought this

Republic into being.

So, make us then to be truly grateful, since we have become heirs of Your special favor. Cause us to have the courage and the wisdom to always seek out and accomplish Your perfect will for each of our lives. And may the power of Your Holy Spirit lead us as dear children to perform Your bidding here upon the earth.

We pray this through the name of Jesus Christ our Lord. Amen."

The Pledge of Allegiance

I had asked Bonnie Auxier Hager to lead us in the pledge to the flag. Bonnie and I had attended Berea College down on the edge of the Bluegrass section of Kentucky some 40 years earlier. I had known that we were related in some way, but genealogy was not a prime interest for me at that time. All I knew was that Bonnie was a "cousin."

I was glad we were using a special flag in this ceremony. It was not difficult to locate a 35 star "Civil War" emblem, and the smaller size I ordered would fit into the custom made case I was having built to display the coat button, shoulder insignia fragment, and coffin nails we had retrieved from David Valentine's grave during the relocation process. 33

The Welcome

Somehow, Dale Carnegie had failed to cover this particular kind of situation when I took his public speaking course twenty-five years earlier. Over the years, I have made strides in conquering stage fright, but almost all of my experiences before audiences had been either in a humorous or a musical setting. I had served as master of ceremony at dozens of banquets and shows, and my wife Eileen and I had sung our

133

---

33 See appendix for a photo of the flag display case.

novelty and folk songs on a regular basis before a variety of audiences. Today's assignment would be more demanding. This was serious business, and I wasn't sure I was up to the task. As I rose and looked over the group before me, which included all five of my living brothers and sisters, my mother, my aunt, and a host of cousins, nephews, and nieces, I gathered my senses as best I could and began to speak.

Author at the 1991 memorial service

"Welcome to this memorial service for Captain David Valentine Auxier, commander of Company A, 39th Kentucky Volunteer Mounted Infantry, U. S. Army, who gave his life in the service of his country on October 4, 1864. I know that some of you have traveled long distances at great expense to be here for this occasion, and I appreciate your presence here today.

My name is also David Auxier, and that is not just a coincidence. I was named after my great, great uncle whom we are honoring in this ceremony. I have heard about David Valentine since I was a child, and it is a fascinating story, indeed. I have tried to imagine the battlefield where he fell, and the cemetery where he was buried, but I never had the opportunity to see those places until last November. My wife Eileen and I were driving through Southwest Virginia and I noticed that the town of Saltville, where David Valentine was buried, was only 11 miles off the interstate highway we were traveling. We decided to take the short side trip to look for his grave site in the McCready Cemetery.

We were lucky to find an old gentleman named Oscar Clear who knew where the cemetery was located. As we approached the area, we were dismayed to see that there was little to identify that there was a cemetery anywhere near. There was no fence, and the graves were overgrown with vines and bushes. David Valentine's grave was not difficult to find because of the handsome military type marker, which had been placed by family members at a memorial service on August 5, 1961.

It became immediately obvious to me that I should look into the possibility of relocating David's remains and markers from that remote and desolate hillside in Virginia to this cemetery where we are gathered today. I feel it is only fitting that David should take his place beside other family members, and especially beside his brother, George Washington Auxier. George was, incidentally, my great, grandfather, who served with David in the war, and who, because of circumstances, was forced to leave him mortally wounded in a farmhouse on the battlefield so long ago.

There was never any question in my mind that relocation to this cemetery was the proper thing to do. It became my objective to convince others in the family. Your presence here today is testimony to the fact that you agreed with me, and I appreciate your support of this project which has become so very important to me.

We seem to be on a 30 year cycle in the recent history of the David Valentine story. As most of you know, the grave site in Virginia was lost until 1931 when two of David's nieces, Mabel Auxier Rice of Paintsville, and Anna Layne Davidson of Prestonsburg, along with their husbands, finally located it after many years of searching by several family members. Then, 30 years later, in 1961, a group of family members dedicated the new marker in the McCready Cemetery. Now, here we are another 30 years later, in 1991, gathered to memorialize David Valentine at what will surely be his final resting place.

I would like to point out that the small fieldstone

inset in concrete at the foot of David's grave is the original stone with "D. AUXIER" inscribed on it, which David's wife, Elizabeth, had placed in the McCready Cemetery in the winter of 1864-65. This stone had fallen over and was almost covered with dirt and leaves when I found it during my initial visit to Saltville.

We are pleased to have with us today, an Honor Guard unit from the 30th Ordnance Detachment at Fort Knox. The unit is under the command of CW3 Donald Kelly, and the Non-commissioned officer in charge is Staff Sergeant S. G. Bethea. Their presentation will conclude this memorial service. I would like to add that the flag they will be folding and presenting today is a copy of the 35 star 'Civil War' flag which was being used at the time of David Valentine was killed in battle.

We are honored to have with us today some friends from Saltville. The people of Saltville and Smyth County, Virginia, have always treated the Auxier family with the utmost respect and courtesy when any of them made trips to search for David's grave, and on subsequent visits to the

Author welcomes Harry Haynes

cemetery. The program of the 1961 memorial service shows that several ladies of the Saltville Chapter of the United Daughters of the Confederacy took part in that service, which proves that old times *can* be forgotten. I certainly found that to be true on my visits to the area.

Mr. Harry Haynes and his wife, Malinda, have driven up from Saltville at my invitation, and I would like you to meet them. Harry helped us with the disinterment in February, and gave us much valuable and interesting information about the battle and the battlefield. He even pointed out the spot where his grandmother told him the Powers family cabin stood,

136

this being the house where David Valentine died. Harry has a very impressive collection of artifacts and relics from the battle at Saltville. I also invited Mr. David Henderson who owns the Henderson Funeral Home which handled the disinterment for us, but he could not be with us today.

I would like to present to you, Harry, this framed display which was built by my brother, Bob, containing one of the buttons from Captain David Valentine's tunic, a nail from the coffin, a picture of the military grave marker, and a write-up about the soldier we are honoring today. The inscription reads as follows: *'Presented to David Henderson and Harry Haynes, and the people of Saltville and Smyth County, for the many kindnesses shown the Auxier family throughout the years. May 26, 1991'"*

Introduction of the Speaker

John David Preston had not yet been born when I left Johnson County in 1948 to attend Berea College. I was 16 years old and had a pretty good idea who all my relatives were in Eastern Kentucky at that time. In the intervening 43 years, most of the older kinfolks passed on, many of the younger ones moved away, and of course, most of the female Auxiers changed their last name. I had visited home several times while Mom and Dad lived on the old farm at Fishtrap, on Paint Creek, but after they moved to Tennessee in 1971, there just was not much to bring me back to the mountains.

When I wrote to Aunt Madge, the only living sibling of my father, Earl Martin Auxier, to apprise her of my plans to move David Valentine's remains, she wrote back that I should contact a cousin named Mary Grace Garland. Mary Grace in turn suggested that I call another cousin named John David Preston, who turned out to be the mayor of Paintsville, the County Seat of Johnson County. This was a fortuitous chain of events because both Mary Grace and John David became key

137

players in the planning and execution of the family reunion and memorial service for David Valentine.

When I met John David for the first time, I was surprised that someone so young had accomplished so much. I asked him about being elected mayor, and with a wry grin, he admitted to using the bold but effective campaign maneuver of publishing the names of every family he was related to in Johnson County. Since the Preston and Auxier names (his mother, Olga, was an Auxier) go all the way back to the early settlement of the Big Sandy Valley, it would be difficult to find a family in that area to whom he was not related.

John David was vitally interested and enthusiastic about the David Valentine relocation project. He had included a fair amount about the Captain in his 1984 book, expanded from a history thesis he wrote while attending Harvard University,. entitled, *"The Civil War in the Big Sandy Valley of Kentucky."* Another connection is that John David is also a great grandson of Major John B. Auxier who organized the first elements of the 39th Kentucky Volunteer Infantry Regiment, in which David Valentine became a company commander. John David had done his homework for this book, and I was impressed by his insightful study of the reasons for the citizens of the Big Sandy Valley choosing sides in the Civil War. The factors and issues were very complex, of course, and some had no clear-cut answers, but I thought the author laid it all out in an interesting and informative manner. The following is the text of my introduction of John David Preston as the principal speaker for the memorial service:

"It is important for every family to occasionally take time to examine its heritage, especially when a member of the family has distinguished himself in some way. We have the perfect opportunity to do that here today as we honor the memory and deeds of Captain David Valentine Auxier.

I can think of no one better qualified to lead us in that examination and in the recapitulation of David

Valentine's story than our speaker today. He is, first of all, one of us, having descended from the Major John B. Auxier line of the family. He was valedictorian of his graduating class at the Prestonsburg, Kentucky High School in 1969. He was graduated magna cum laude with a bachelor's degree in history from Harvard University in 1973. He is a 1976 law graduate of the University of Kentucky, and has been a practicing attorney in Paintsville, Kentucky since 1976.

John David Preston

Our speaker was Commonwealth's Attorney of the 24th Judicial Circuit from 1982 to 1987, and was elected Mayor of the City of Paintsville in 1988. He is a life member of the Ashland, Kentucky, Chapter of the Kentucky Sons of the American Revolution, and is a charter member of the Big Sandy Historical Society. He is a historian in his own right, having written and published a book entitled 'The Civil War in the Big Sandy Valley of Kentucky.'

He is married to the former Mary Avonne Stephenson of Snyder, New York, and they have one daughter, Ellen Marie, age 7 months. They are members of the Mayo Methodist Church in Paintsville.

It is with pleasure that I introduce to you at this time, my cousin, the Honorable John David Preston."

The Address (paraphrased from video)

"How does one condense a man's life into a 20 minute presentation? Since we know very little of David Valentine Auxier's early childhood and developmental years, any narrative about him is necessarily going to be concentrated on the events occurring in the last two years of his life. There was an abundance of action in those two years.

We know that Captain David Valentine Auxier was born April 30, 1840 at the Mouth of John's Creek in the Blockhouse Bottom in Johnson County, Kentucky. His father was Nathaniel Auxier and his mother was Hester Ann Mayo Auxier. David Valentine was named after his mother's grandfather, Valentine Mayo. David was the second oldest of 13 children. We know from his enlistment papers that he was five feet seven inches tall, had dark complexion, black hair, and black eyes. His occupation was listed as 'tanner.' He was married to Elizabeth Hinton of Greenup County, Kentucky, on August 2, 1864, just two months before he was killed.

David enlisted in the 39th Kentucky Volunteer Infantry, US Army, on September 6, 1862, at Peach Orchard in Lawrence County. His uncle, John B. Auxier, had organized a group of neighbors and friends into a company of militia as a means of protecting against marauding bands of Confederates who were in the valley from time to time.

Soon after his enlistment, David was elected [3rd] Lieutenant of his company. I use the word 'elected' because at that time, the men chose their own officers. David would later be joined by his younger brother, George Washington, who was elected Sergeant.

The regiment was not officially mustered into the US Army until February 18, 1863, but David Valentine was not with his company at that time because he was in confinement in the state penitentiary of Virginia in Richmond. He and several others of his unit had been captured by Virginia State Line troopers on December 4, 1862 at Wireman's Shoals on the Big Sandy River in Floyd County. The battle, also known as 'The Boat Fight' by local historians, was disastrous for the Federals because they not only lost 2 killed and 25 captured, but lost ammunition and quartermaster supplies valued at $250,000.00.

Lieutenant Auxier was one of those captured, along with Lieutenant Isaac Goble, the husband of one of his cousins, and the prisoners were tied together with ropes and force-marched to a railroad connection where they were transported to Richmond, Virginia. Their captors had not yet aligned with the Confederacy, so David and his comrades were not considered prisoners of war as such. Therefore, they were not eligible for exchange under the cartel, which was in effect between the US Army and the Army of the Confederacy, and as a result, were held in 'close confinement' in the Virginia state penitentiary instead of the notorious Libby Confederate prison in Richmond.

Coincidentally, the North was holding a Southern Colonel named Richard Thomas, alias Richard Thomas Zarvona, in Fort Lafayette in New York harbor. Zarvona, who became known as the 'French Lady' because of his penchant for dressing up in women's clothing to accomplish his spy and piracy activities, had been captured in the Chesapeake Bay area after seizing a Union steamboat. The Zarvona case had gained much notoriety, and since the Colonel was Virginia militia instead of Confederate Army, he too, was ineligible for the usual prisoner of war exchange program.

David Valentine immediately started a letter writing campaign from prison to try to effect an exchange for himself and six of his buddies, for Colonel Zarvona. Family members have some of David's original letters, and there are copies of other letters to his father, Nathaniel, his congressman, Secretary of War Edwin Stanton, and one letter from Virginia Governor John Letcher to President Abraham Lincoln concerning the proposed exchange. Finally, a deal was struck and David and his comrades were released from the

Richmond prison on May 5, 1863. They walked back to Eastern Kentucky, a distance of some 400 miles, and rejoined their unit.

Records show that David's regiment was involved in several skirmishes during the following 18 months. These were all in Eastern Kentucky, Southwest Virginia, and along the border of West Virginia, which had split off and become a state of its own in June, 1863. It was on one of these assignments that David probably met Elizabeth Hinton. They were married on August 2, 1864.

The most important battle of the war involving soldiers of the Big Sandy Valley took place on October 2, 1864 at the town of Saltville in Smyth County, Virginia. Saltville was important to the Confederacy because of the huge amount of salt produced there. There being no refrigeration at that time, salt was necessary for preservation of meat for the army. The vats boiled day and night, processing as much as 10,000 bushels of salt daily.

General Stephen Gano Burbridge, with approximately 4,200 Union troops in 12 regiments, approached Saltville from the North on Sunday morning, October 2. The Confederates had a very small garrison of only about 400 men, but Southern sympathizers from Kentucky had ridden ahead to warn of the impending raid, and by 9:30 a.m., the defenders had gathered forces numbering approximately 2,700 men.

The fight raged all day, but despite superior numbers, the Union could not dislodge the Rebels from the slopes and hilltops overlooking the North Fork of the Holston River that flowed through the little town of Saltville. General Burbridge, his troops exhausted and out of ammunition, ordered a 'withdrawal' back across the mountains to Kentucky, leaving some 350 dead and wounded on the battlefield.

One of those left behind was David Valentine Auxier, wounded by a bullet through his right lung. His brother, Sergeant George Washington, Auxier, and his uncle, Major John B. Auxier, found David after the battle, and agonized over having to leave him, but David insisted they go for their own safety. He died two days later and was buried on the Powers farm near where he fell. Later that winter, David's wife, Elizabeth, accompanied by a family friend and Southern sympathizer named Robert Hurt, went to Saltville, located her husband's grave, and had his remains moved to a family cemetery in the little community of McCready, where David's regiment had been in action. A small fieldstone with 'D. AUXIER' inscribed on it was placed on the grave at that time.

Elizabeth Hinton Auxier made one more trip to the McCready cemetery after the war, this time accompanied by David's uncle, James E. Stewart. Elizabeth then moved back to Greenup County, remarried, and in time, the location of David's grave in Virginia was lost to the Auxier family.

Over the ensuing years, various attempts were made to find the grave- site, but all were unsuccessful until 1931, when two of David's nieces, Mabel Auxier Rice and Anna Layne Davidson, found an old man named Curren Sanders who remembered the grieving young widow from Kentucky. He directed the nieces to the McCready Cemetery where they located the long lost headstone of their ancestor. In 1961, the Saltville Chapter of the United Daughters of the Confederacy took part in the ceremony at which Auxier relatives dedicated a new bronze military marker for the grave.

There were over 600,000 casualties in the Civil War, and Captain David Valentine Auxier was only one of them, but we honor him today because he symbolizes all those who served and those who died in that terrible conflict which divided our nation so many years ago. As fine a place as Southwest Virginia is, and it truly is a wonderful area, I believe David Valentine would be better satisfied to be buried in his native soil among his own people. I am proud and pleased that he has finally come home."

The Placing of the Wreath

I had not met Mary Grace Garland before our arrival at Paintsville with David Valentine's remains, just three months earlier. 34 I had known about her through relatives, and had a brief telephone conversation with her once, but I was more familiar with the name of her mother, Mabel Auxier Rice, who was among those who searched for and found David Valentine's grave at Saltville. Mabel and her husband, Garland Rice, were vitally interested in family history and genealogy, and their names had appeared numerous times in my research.

Mary Grace and I are the same number of generations removed from our Civil War uncle David Valentine, and since her mother had placed the wreath at the dedication of the new marker at the grave site at Saltville 30 years earlier, I thought it only proper that Mary Grace should have the same honor at this ceremony. There had been an "In Memoriam" given at Saltville, but for our service today, we decided to eliminate that as a separate function, and simply combine it with the placing of the wreath.

Mary Grace
Garland

I suggested to Mary Grace that she compose her own

---

34 At the memorial service planning meeting, Mary Grace showed us a piece of the buffalo hide given to Sarah, wife of Samuel Auxier, by Daniel Boone in the winter of 1796-97. Mary Grace is now deceased.

speech for presentation, or in lieu of that, she could use the same one given by her mother at the 1961 service. It turned out that Mary Grace was a no-nonsense lady who believed in getting right to the point. As she made her way to the grave, she turned to the assembled group and said the following:

> "I place this wreath at the grave of our honored ancestor who has come home to be among his Auxier kin."

The Honor Guard Ceremony

The seven member rifle squad of the 30th Ordnance Detachment Honor Guard from Ft. Knox had been standing at parade rest in a gravel roadbed some 50 yards from the tents during the 45 minute ceremony. The sun bore down on them relentlessly, and I agonized for them in their winter uniforms. Having spent two years in the Army, I was aware that the military had strict rules about when to change from winter to summer uniforms. I vaguely remembered that it was June 1st, which would have been 5 days hence. The presentation would have been no less impressive to me if the men had been in short sleeve shirts instead of their heavy, long sleeve jackets.

I was so pleased and proud that the honor guard was actually there to close the memorial service. Even though the application had been made at the Casualty Office at Ft. Knox many weeks earlier, there was the problem that they would not make a commitment to come to Johnson County until three days before the date. I understood their reasons, but at the same time, I wanted *our* ceremony to be perfect. It would not be perfect without the distinctiveness and prestige of the honor guard.

The planning committee and I had gone through a lot of "what-if's" concerning the uncertainty of the guard being present. The program had to be printed well before the three day time limit imposed by the Ft. Knox Casualty Office, and what if we listed the guard as a part of the program and they were unable to be present? John David Preston's back-up plan to ask some Union Army re-enactors to come and fire muskets over the grave had fallen through, but even if he had secured such a unit, they would have no one to blow "Taps" or fold and present the flag.

I was still fretting over the supposition that the Ft. Knox detachment could not furnish a bugler. What would a military honor guard ceremony be without a bugler? So I implored them to borrow one from Ft. Campbell or some other post in the region. They rebutted that all the other units were assigned because of the heavy Memorial Day weekend activities.

After Mary Grace had placed the wreath and returned to the tents, Warrant Officer Donald Kelly, the officer-in-charge, touched the bill of his hat as a signal to Staff Sergeant S. G. Bethea, and the order was given to come to attention in preparation for the twenty-one gun salute. Every eye was riveted on the men in uniform

Honor guard detail

as they assumed the firing position and squeezed off three rounds from the seven rifles at precise intervals. And then, to my overwhelming surprise and delight, I heard one of the most glorious sounds of my life. From a grove of trees in a far corner of the cemetery came the haunting strains of a lone bugler playing the traditional military funeral call. How could such a miracle be happening? We could not see behind the trees, and I wondered if perhaps the musician had arrived at the last moment without his uniform.

The shock of hearing this beautiful and perfectly played rendition, after the disappointment of being told we would not have it, was almost too much for me. I was glad I was on the front row of the tents so that those behind me could not see the tears that began to flow. My lower lip had a mind of its own, and I am sure my body must have swayed from the perpendicular as the last notes from the bugle drifted over the hushed crowd. I said a silent thanks for having planned the program so that I would not have to say anything at this juncture. My emotions would simply not have permitted it. I was aware of the sound of sniffling and blowing of noses from the rows behind me. I chose not to change positions until I regained my composure.

Sergeant Bethea gave a command and the soldiers knelt on one knee and placed their rifles on the ground in front of them. In a moment they were marching in lockstep down the slope to the front of the tent where the "Civil War" flag was fluttering in the soft breeze. Taking their positions facing each other in two ranks, the flag was removed and ceremoniously folded in a succession of overlapping triangles as Warrant Officer Kelly stood at rigid attention at one end of the formation. The process took a little longer than normal because this particular flag was somewhat smaller than the standard casket size banner the unit was used to handling.

The flag was carefully and lovingly passed between the opposing ranks of soldiers, each pair making their share of folds, until it arrived in a neat and compact bundle in the hands of the final twosome. Just before this part of the ceremony was finished, an object was placed inside the flag. I later learned that it is an honor guard tradition to place a casing from the 21 gun salute inside the final fold of the flag.

Folding the flag

Officer Kelly took the flag and walked briskly in my direction. He bent down, placed the folded banner in my hands and said in a voice that was almost a whisper:

"On behalf of the President of the United States and a grateful nation, I present to you this National Flag as a token of the honorable and faithful service rendered by your loved one to this nation."

A snappy salute from Officer Kelly and the ceremony was over It was then that I learned that the "Taps" we had listened to was a recording played back on a cassette tape concealed behind the trees. It made no difference to me that it was canned, but they could have allayed much of my anxiety if they had told me three days earlier that they could do it that way.

CWO Kelly presents the flag to the author

I was relieved that our final tribute to David Valentine Auxier was concluded, and I was still a bit shaky as the two television stations did on-camera interviews with John David Preston and me. I don't even remember the questions or what my answers were. *The Paintsville Herald* printed a full page spread on the David Valentine relocation and memorial service. It was a nice closure for a story that spanned more than twelve decades. This was ***DAVID VALENTINE'S DAY***.

Dave and his wife Eileen with David Valentine's military
marker at its new and final location in the Johnson County
Memorial Cemetery at Staffordsville, KY

EPILOGUE

There you have it folks. My twenty year literary odyssey into the life and persona of my great, great uncle, Captain David Valentine Auxier, U.S.A., and my ethereal relationship to him, are finished. I feel a weight has been lifted from my shoulders and psyche because of the profound obligation I felt to write this book. First of all, I do not take lightly the honor that I was named after David Valentine. Secondly, I needed to repay a karmic debt to David Valentine and to my great grandfather, George Washington Auxier, David's brother who, due to the exigencies of the situation, had to leave David mortally wounded on a battlefield in Virginia. As I explained in Chapter II, George and I have much in common, and I feel that in many ways, I am the present day embodiment of my ancestor.

Thirdly, I know that many of my cousins know at least a smattering of our family hero's story, and hopefully will appreciate a detailed history of his life and who he was as a man, as a citizen, and as a soldier who gave his life for a cause in which he truly believed. I sincerely hope I have fulfilled that mission with this biography.

I will close with a dream I had on the night of November 8, 2009, which affirms my conviction that the relocation of David Valentine's remains from the abandoned cemetery in Virginia, and the two decade project of writing this book was the right and proper thing to do. I had just returned from a spiritual study retreat in Tennessee which focused on meditation and dream interpretation.

The Dream

I had assembled a group of people to help me disinter the remains of someone who had been dead a very long time. There was not a "grave," as such, but there was a large vault which contained a black metal casket and several musical instrument cases, presumably containing guitars, banjos, fiddles, etc. I opened the casket, and inside was a large leather bag with a zipper fastener. I unzipped it, and found another smaller bag, and another inside it, and so on until I got to the last one. There was no body. Nothing! In the dream, I got the feeling that I had been through this process before. My son, Randy, who helped me with David Valentine's original exhumation in Virginia in 1990, remarked that the small doll that had been there with the body previously, was now missing as well. During this process of opening the vault and bags, I experienced several tremendous jolts of energy up and down my spine. We zipped up all the bags and closed the casket and vault. I did not open any of the instrument cases. *End of dream.*

As I was lying in bed after the dream, still in a half-awake state, I remembered what the presenter had taught us at the retreat about interpreting dreams. He had instructed us to not move a muscle while processing the dream. I lay perfectly still, thinking this was definitely a message of some kind about David Valentine, and I began to smile.

My Interpretation

I concluded that this was a replay of the 1991 relocation of David Valentine's remains to his family graveyard in Kentucky. The succession of leather bags inside the casket represented the several generations that had passed since David's death in 1864. The small "voodoo" type doll was David Valentine's spirit which I had transplanted to his new grave in Kentucky. I had in effect, released his spirit from his all-but-forgotten tomb in Virginia. The energy jolts told me I was onto something really significant.

I was happy with my interpretation. Then I had another enlightenment! I remembered the musical instrument cases in the vault and wondered what they represented. As far as we know, David Valentine was not musical, but his brother George, my great-grandfather *was!* He loved to sing and play the banjo and fiddle, just as I love to sing and play the guitar and banjo today. Along with other similarities, I am in many ways a template for George as he was in his adult life. I truly believe that I am my own great grandfather. There, I said it!

This revelation about the musical instrument cases begs the question: "Was the released spirit that of David Valentine or my great-grandfather George?" After pondering that uncertainty at length, I have concluded that it really doesn't matter. The burden has been lifted and I can get on with the rest of my earthly sojourn in peace, with that karmic monkey no longer perched on my back.

BILBLIOGRAPHY

Auxier, Agnes Masolete. *Auxier History: One Branch, 1755-1908*, With additions and corrections by John Earl Atkinson. Unpublished typescript, approx. 100 pp.,1952. (In possession of the author; various other copies held in the Auxier family).

-------------. Addendum [1] to Agnes Auxier's *Auxier History: One Branch, 1755-1908*. Unknown author. About 1960. (Typescript in possession of the author).

-------------. Addendum [2] to Agnes Auxier's *Auxier History: One Branch, 1755-1908. The Herald Advertiser,* Huntington, WV. Jan. 27, 1963. (Typescript in possession of the author).

-------------. Addendum [3] to Agnes Auxier's A*uxier History: One Branch, 1755-1908*. The Paintsville Herald, Paintsville, KY, August 21, 1963. (Typescript in possession of the author).

Auxier, Dave, *The Auxier Family.* Dexter, MI: Thompson-Shore, Inc., 1995.

Auxier, Dave and Need, Judith Tickel. *The Auxier Family 2nd ed.* Dexter, MI: Thompson-Shore, Inc., 2000.

Baker, Robert M. and Hall, Brian E., *The 39th Kentucky Mounted Infantry, U.S. Volunteers,* CD-ROM, Bushwhacker Books, London, KY, 1999 – 2000.

Bowman, John S. *The Civil War Day by Day,* Dorset Press, Greenwich, CT, 1989.
Connelley, William Elsey. *The Founding of Harman's Station,* Westminster, MD: A facsilimile reprint by Heritage Books, 2006. (Originally published 1910 by William Elsey Connelley)

Dyer, Frederick H. *Compendium of the War of the Rebellion, Part III*. Thomas Yoseleff, NY, 1959. (Originally published Des Moines, IA: The Dyer Publishing Co., 1908).

Ely, William. *The Big Sandy Valley*. Cattlettsburg,Kentucky, Central Methodist. 1887.

Filson Historical Society. *Abraham Lincoln and Emancipation in Kentucky*. Filson Historical Society website.

Foster, Stephen T .Explanation of the prisoner exchange cartel implemented in the early stages of the Civil War. Paper presented to the Memphis (TN) Metal Detector Club, 1995.

Galbraith, Douglas Auxier. Revisions and Additions to *Auxier Family History: One Branch, 1755 –1908*. (Undated typescript in possession of author), 1940's.

Garrison, Webb. *Civil War Hostages: Hostage Taking in the Civil War*. Shippensburg, PA: White Mane Books, 2000.

Hall, C. Mitchell. *Jenny Wiley Country: A History of "Jenny Wiley Country" and Genealogy of Its People up to the Year 1984*. Volume 4. Washington, D.C.: Published by Author, 1985.

Hesseltine, William B. *Civil War Prisons*. Frederick Ungar Publishing Co., NY: White Mane Books, 1930.
Kentucky Historical Society, Military History Museum, Frankfort, KY. Voucher Form 12, State of Kentucky, dated Sept. 25, Dec. 4, 1862; Jan. 6, Feb. 12, 1863. (Copies in possession of the author).

Marsh, Robert L. "A Brief History of Johnson County, Kentucky," in *Johnson County Kentucky History and Families*. Eds. Keith Steele and Dave Turner. Paducah, KY: Turner Publishing Co., 2001 (pp. 8-21).

Marvel, William. *Southwest Virginia in the Civil War: The Battles for Saltville.* Lynchburg, VA: H.E. Howard, Inc., 1992.

Mays, Thomas D. *The Saltville Massacre.* Ft. Worth, TX: Ryan Place Publishers, 1995.

Morgan, Robert. *Boone: A Biography.* Chapel Hill, NC: Algonquin Books of Chapel Hill, 2008

Paintsville Herald, The. *Pioneer Settlement Cradles Beyond "Scouting Ground."* Paintsville, KY. Jan. 7, 1959. (Typescript in possession of the author).

Pelzer, John D. and Pelzer, Linda C. *Zarvona, The French Lady.* The Civil War Times Illustrated. May/June 1992.

Preston, John David. *The Civil War in the Big Sandy Valley of Kentucky.* 2nd ed. Baltimore: Gateway Press, Inc., 2008.

Prisoner of War Records, Dept. of Military Affairs, Commonwealth of Kentucky, Frankfort, KY. Memorandum Issued at City Point, VA. Dated May 7,1863. (Copy in possession of the author).
Rice, Garland H. *Memorial Service, Captain David Valentine Auxier. Aug 5, 1961. (*Program in possession of the author).

Rice, Mary Louise. *Biographical Sketches and Records.* Dec. 12, 1926. (Typescript in possession of the author).

Scalf, Henry P. *"Captain David Valentine Auxier, U.S.A. (1840-1864)."* Monograph privately printed by the author, n.d. Reprint of *"Civil War Bitterness Flowered when East Kentuckians Fought,"* in Floyd County Times. Prestonsburg, KY: April 13, 1961.

------------. *Our Memories of the Civil War Linger.* Address to United Daughters of the Confederacy, Oct. 8, 1971. Prestonsburg, KY. (Typescript in possession of the author).

------------. *Stephen Meek Ferguson, Lt. Col. of 39th Kentucky Volunteer Regiments, U.S.A.* Prestonsburg, KY: Statewide Press, 1962.

Strassburger, Ralph B. *Pennsylvania German Pioneers.* Norristown, PA, 1934.

Trudeau, Noah Andre. *Like Men of War: Black Troops in the Civil War, 1862-1865.* Edison, NJ: Castle Books, 2002.

United States Pension Office, *Widow's Claim for Pension, Elizabeth S. Childs,* Jan 25, 1866. (Copy in possession of the author).

------------. *Affidavit of C. T. Wilson.* Jackson County, WV April 29, 1905. (No case number marked) (Copy in possession of the author).

------------. *Affidavit of County Clerk G. B. Crow,* Jackson Co., WV, Aug 14, 1905. (No case number marked) (Copy in possession of the author).

-----------. *Affidavit of Elizabeth S. Chase. W.O. 89.409, W.Ct. 87.649,* Jan. 2, 1903 (Copy in possession of the author).

------------. *Affidavit of Isaac Goble, Floyd Co., KY. Stamped by U.S. Pension Office Jan. 8, 1906. (No case number marked). (*Copy in possession of the author).

------------. *Deposition of Dr. Isaac Goble, U.S. Pension Office, Case No. 364.427.* Mar. 20, 1883. (Copy in possession of the author).

-----------. *Statement of County Court Clerk, Jackson Co., WV,* Jun. 9, 1904. (No case number marked). (Copy in possession of the author).

Walker, Gary C. *The War in Southwest Virginia, 1861-1865.* 5th ed., revised. Roanoke, VA: Gurtner Printing Co., 1985.

War of the Rebellion, The: A Compilation of Official Records of the Union and Confederate Armies. Series I, vols, XXXII, XXXIX; Series II, vols. II, V. United States Government: Washington, D.C., 1902.

Wells, Charles C. *Kentucky Archives, Johnson County Vital Statistics 1843–1904* Gateway Press, Inc.: Baltimore, MD, 1993.

Wells, John Britton, III. *From Armsheim to Auxier: The Odyssey of the American Auxier Family.* (Issued from Newnan, GA, 2001). (Unpublished typescript in possession of the author).

------------. *The Axer/Oxier/Auxier Family: From Albig to Auxier* (Issued from Newnan, GA, 2005). (Unpublished typescript in possession of the author).

------------. *The Axer/Auxer/ Oxier/Auxier Family: From Rheydt to Auxier.,* (Issued from Newnan, GA, June 15, 2006). (Unpublished typescript in possession of the author).

------------. Letter to Judith Tickel Need. *Auxier family members who served in the Confederate Army during the Civil War.* November 6, 1998. (Copy in possession of the author).

Wolford, George. *Lawrence County: A Pictoral History,* Ashland, KY: 1972.

APPENDIX

Numerous purchase orders from Col. John Dils of the 39th Kentucky Volunteers to the State of Kentucky at this period of time immediately before and after the "boat fight" show requests for payment to various suppliers of goods and services. Among these were (1) The use of push boats out of Cattlettsburg, KY, for 124 1/2 days @ $1.00/day each; (2) The service of 49 men for 18 1/2 days, totaling $629.50; (3) The boarding and lodging of seven sick soldiers for 40 days @ 40 cents/day, totaling $112.00; (4) The purchase of 65 1/2 bushels of wheat @ $1.00/bushel and 100 bushels of corn @ 50 cents/bushel from Samuel Auxier, Jr., David Valentine's grandfather; (5) The purchase of 60 bushels of wheat @ $1.00/bushel and 500 pounds of bacon @ 8 cents/lb from Benjamin Franklin Auxier, David Valentine's cousin, and (6) other invoices for beef @ 3 1/2 cents/lb, flour @ 3 cents/lb, meal @ 60 cents/lb., and potatoes @ $1.00/bushel. (KHS)

Some of the invoices for these purchases and other goods and services are reproduced on the following pages, along with numerous documents pertaining to the David Valentine story:

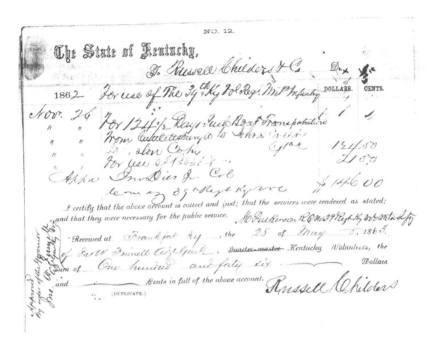

Push Boat rental invoice for the 39th KY Vol. Inf.

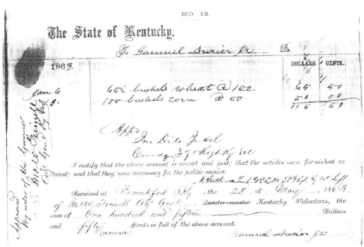

Samuel Auxier invoice for wheat and corn

Ben Auxier invoice for wheat and bacon

Alexander Smiley invoice for push boat labor

A. C. Hutchison invoice for lodging sick soldiers

of the 39th KY Volunteer Infantry

Dr. James Hereford payment voucher

Muster-in roll of the 39th KY Volunteer Infantry

165

Muster Roll of the 39th KY Volunteer Infantry

Prisoner of War memorandum

about David Valentine Auxier

166

Marriage bond for Capt. David Valentine Auxier
and Elizabeth Hinton, August 2, 1864

167

Marriage certificate for Capt. David Valentine Auxier
and Elizabeth Hinton, August 2, 1864

DVA letter to his father Nathaniel, from prison,

April 7, 1863

DVA letter to his cousin Angeline Prater,
July 18, 1863

170

DVA letter to his cousin Angeline Prater,

Aug. 9, 1863

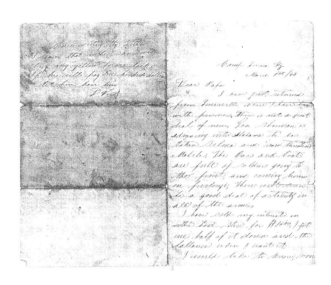

DVA letter to Papa, Mar. 1, 1864

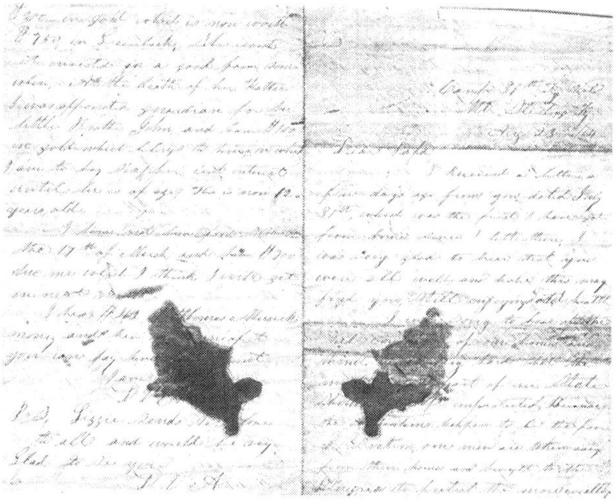

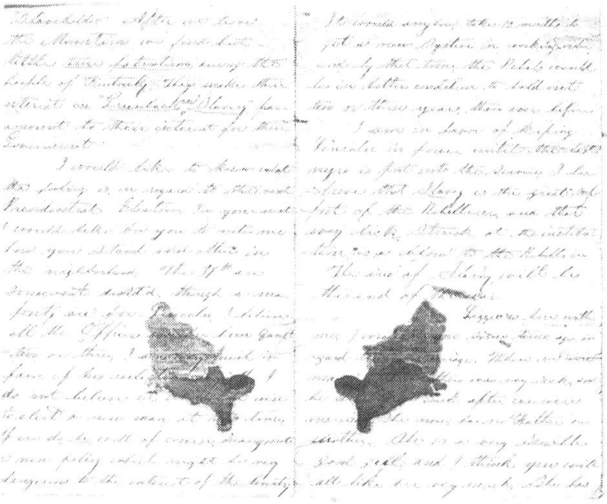

DVA letter to Papa, Aug. 23, 1864

DVA letter to his cousin Angeline Prater,

Aug. 29, 1864

TO WHOM IT MAY CONCERN:

Permission is hereby granted for
the erection of a Marker at the grave of David
W Auxier, a revolutionary soldier, in the Mc
Cready cemetary- Located near McCready Post
Office - Virginia.
This the 21 day of November 1953

Mrs W J Talbert-
Nearest of kin to owner.

Witness:

Ernest I McCready
Grandson-

Permit to install 1961 DVA grave marker,

Nov 21, 1953

U. S. F. & G. INTER-OFFICE CORRESPONDENCE

TO: Geo W Auxier-   DATE: 11-25-'53
FROM: G. H. Rice
SUBJECT: Permit-

Enclosed find permit of Mrs W J Talbert a daughter
of owner (who is now deceased) also grandson who
is employed in Post Office at Saltville, Va.- the
McCready Office has been abolished.- You may have
markers sent to him Ernest I McCready, Saltville, Va-
He is very anxious to assist- therefore you may get in
touch with him any time he can be of assistance- If applications are to be executed, he will assist-
If you will give to me the size of bronze plaque with appropriate inscription- I will try to arrange for same-
Martha is somewhat improved, but yet in hospital- other-
wise all are well-

Permit to ship DVA grave marker to Saltville,

Nov. 25, 1953

175

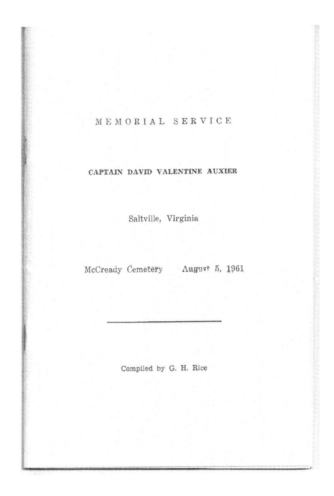

MEMORIAL SERVICE

CAPTAIN DAVID VALENTINE AUXIER

Saltville, Virginia

McCready Cemetery   August 5, 1961

Compiled by G. H. Rice

Saltville Memorial Service Program Cover,

Aug. 5, 1961

176

PRAYER BY RUTH DAVIDSON SOWARDS AT THE GRAVESIDE MEMORIAL
SERVICE FOR CAPT. DAVID VALENTINE AUXIER AT THE MCCREADY
CEMETERY, SALTVILLE, VIRGINIA. AUGUST 5, 1961

OUR FATHER IN HEAVEN, WE THANK THEE FOR THY GUIDANCE
AND FOR THY ABIDING PRESENCE IN THE LIFE OF OUR COUNTRY.

WE THANK THEE FOR ALL THOSE YESTERYEARS OF OUR HUMAN
RACE WHOSE FULFILMENTS HAVE BECOME A HERITAGE TO US.

GUIDE US ALL TO PATHS OF PEACE IN THESE PERILOUS DAYS,
AND MAY THY GUIDING PRESENCE BE EVER NEAR.

WE GIVE THEE THANKS FOR THE GOOD EXAMPLES OF THY
SERVANT WHO, HAVING FINISHED HIS COURSE IN FAITH AND
SERVICE, NOW RESTS FROM HIS LABORS.

WE ARE GRATEFUL, DEAR LORD, FOR THE FORBEARS WHO
BEQUEATHED TO US A GLORIOUS HERITAGE. KEEP EVER IN OUR
MINDS AND HEARTS A SPIRIT OF FERVENT GRATITUDE. GIVE US
LOVE, UNDERSTANDING, PATIENCE, AND COURAGE, THAT WE MAY
AT ALL TIMES BE WORTHY OF THY BLESSINGS.

WE THANK THEE, DEAR LORD, FOR THY GUIDANCE IN LEADING US
TO OUR DEAR FRIEND, MISS MINNIE FRYE, WHO MADE IT POSSIBLE
TO FIND THE GRAVE OF OUR LOVED ONE, AND TO ERNEST
McCREADY, WHO HAS SO UNTIRINGLY ASSISTED IN MAKING THIS
DAY A MEMORABLE ONE.

BE PRESENT AMONG US, WE PRAY, AS ON THIS DAY WE
ENDEAVOR TO MEET THE CHALLENGE OF THE HOUR. GUIDE US IN
EVERY THOUGHT AND DEED TO THY HONOR AND GLORY.

AMEN

Prayer given by Ruth Davidson Sowards at the 1961 Memorial Service for David Valentine Auxier at Saltville, VA

Transit permit for moving DVA's
remains from Saltville, VA, to Kentucky, Feb. 6, 1991

STATEMENT

Paintsville Funeral Home

P. O. Box 194 :: Second St.
Telephone 789-5123
PAINTSVILLE, KY. 41240

Dr. C. O. Auxier

2121 Elvis Presley Blvd.

Memphis, Tennessee   38106

DATE	DESCRIPTION	BALANCE
	BALANCE BROUGHT FORWARD	
2-12-91	Interment of David Valentine Auxier in Johnson County Memorial, Staffordsville, Kentucky	$100.00

Feb. 20, 1991 paid in full by cash

Julia Preston

Re-interment fee for DVA's remains in

Johnson County Memorial Cemetery, Feb. 12, 1991

179

STATEMENT

Johnson Co. Memorial, Inc.

P.O. Box 661
Paintsville, Ky. 41240

Dr. C. D. Auxier
2034 Elvis Presley Blvd.
Memphis, Tennessee 38106

Quantity	Description	Balance
	BALANCE BROUGHT FORWARD	
2-19-91	Re-interment of David Valentine Auxier Block 4, Plot 23	$325.00

Feb. 2d 1991
paid in full by
Check C.D. auxier

Eugene Sturgill

Re-interment fee for DVA's remains in

Johnson Co. Memorial Cemetery, Feb. 19, 1991

180

DEPARTMENT OF THE ARMY
U.S. TOTAL ARMY PERSONNEL COMMAND
ALEXANDRIA, VA
22331-0482

November 26, 1993

Mortuary Affairs and Casualty
Support Division

Doctor C. D. Auxier
2034 Elvis Presley Blvd
Memphis, Tennessee 38106

Dear Dr. Auxier:

    Your claim for reimbursement of disinterment expenses for your
great uncle, Captain David V. Auxier, has been approved for payment
in the amount of $925.00. You will receive a check for this amount
in the near future.

    My sympathy remains with you in the loss of your loved one.

                              Sincerely,

                              Harold W. Campbell
                              Chief, Disposition Branch
                              Mortuary Affairs and Casualty
                                  Support Division

Reimbursement letter, Dept. of the Army,

Nov. 24, 1993

Author's custom made walnut display case containing the flag used at the May 26, 1991 honor guard memorial service for David Valentine Auxier. Included in the display are a set of authentic Civil War Captain's shoulder insignia, a photo of DVA and his bronze military grave marker, and bullets retrieved from the Saltville battlefield. It also includes items retrieved from the grave during the relocation of his remains to Kentucky, including one of the infantry officer's buttons from David's tunic with the cloth backing for some of the buttons, a nail from the coffin, and a small section of his braided Captain's insignia superimposed on a picture of the full insignia..